WALKING
NORTHERN
RAILWAYS

VOL.I. EAST

Viaduct over the River Lune beyond Mickleton.
Barnard Castle-Middleton in Teesdale line.

WALKING NORTHERN RAILWAYS

VOL.I. EAST

Charlie Emett

Maps and Photography by David Bell

CICERONE PRESS,
MILNTHORPE, CUMBRIA

© Charlie Emett 1986
ISBN 0902 363 76 X
First Published 1986

CONTENTS

INTRODUCTION

North Eastern England is not Paradise. Paradise suggests an idealised landscape, Utopia, a never-never land. It is a product of the human imagination and probably exists nowhere on earth.

Over the last two centuries England has been transformed from a predominantly rural and agricultural community to a crowded industrial and technological society. North Eastern England, largely because of its rich deposits of coal and other minerals, became deeply involved in the Industrial Revolution; and as a result great tracts of land, particularly on and around the coal fields, became despoiled. Much ugliness remains although today much landscaping is being carried out. Many pit heaps have vanished altogether while others have been transformed into pleasing shapes, seeded and planted with trees. Heavy industry and shipbuilding have, by their very nature, produced ugly rashes on the landscape and this has made the remote and wilder places more attractive.

The North East is often depicted as a great wasteland with huge spoil heaps stretching into infinity. This view, usually expressed with authority by those who have never been near the place, is a false one. In reality the North East, despite its industrialisation, has a great deal of beauty and interest to offer the discerning visitor.

The Glorious Twelfth, red grouse and purple heather; the vast, rolling North York Moors (a National park since 1952); the bleak, gritstone fells; the long, lovely dales and the quiet villages, sturdily built of natural stone around hoary old churches are as much a part of the North East as the I.C.I. complex at Teeside.

On a headland in a loop of the River Wear there stands Durham, the most magnificently sited of all English cathedrals. Here, at this splendid Norman edifice, is enough beauty and solemn grandeur to satisfy the most exacting. Durham town, however, is not an attractive place for where coal is to be won natural beauty must be sacrificed.

It is in the western parts of Durham and in Teesdale in particular that the county's most charming of scenery lies. There, above Middleton, is a wide and lovely dale dotted with whitewashed farms and bounded by high fells. There, too, stands High Force, the proudest waterfall in all England; and higher up, the glistening, ebony, rocky staircase of Cauldron Snout down which the foaming infant Tees plunges. In this region Durham is blessed with scenery as wild and desolate as any in England.

Northumberland, the most northerly English county, and part of the ancient kingdom of Northumbria, flavours the great appeal of its countryside with many mementoes of its wild and stirring past. Scarred masonry on its grim castles and pele towers testifies to a turbulent past.

Its shore is long, windswept and lonely with many splendid sandy beaches and fine curving bays.

A dozen miles south of Berwick, on Holy Island, Lindisfarne Castle sits on a whinstone outcrop. On the mainland, across Budle Bay from the island, ancient Bamburgh Castle proudly straddles a huge basalt rock, while not far away Dunstanburgh Castle, perhaps the greatest Northumbrian castle of them all, lies ruinous: an honourable trio, resolute guardians of Northumberland's rich heritage.

Inland, on the northern marches, the Cheviots, with their lovely glens and fast flowing streams, beckon to seekers of solitude and quiet places.

To the south of the county, Hadrians' Wall invites enthusiasts to walk in the steps of the Romans.

The North East offers something for everyone. Good hostelries abound, local breweries produce potent brews and the locals are friendly.

But where exactly *is* the North East? For the purpose of this book it is an irregular triangle of land with its base joining Leeds to Hull, its western side joining Leeds to Berwick via Hawes, Kirkby Stephen, Alston, Lambley and Woodburn and its eastern side being the coast from Hull to Berwick. All the walks along the abandoned railways presented here lie within this rough triangle. I have divided the North East into four areas:-

I North Yorkshire and North Humberside
An area bounded on the east by the coast between Hull and Saltburn, on the south by an imaginary line between Hull and Selby, on the north by an imaginary line between Saltburn and Darlington and on the west by that part of the main London to Edinburgh railway line between Darlington and Selby.

II West and North West Yorkshire
An area bounded on the west by an imaginary line between Leeds and Kirkby Stephen, on the south by an imaginary line between Leeds and Selby, on the north by the closed line between Kirkby Stephen and Darlington and on the east by that part of the main London to

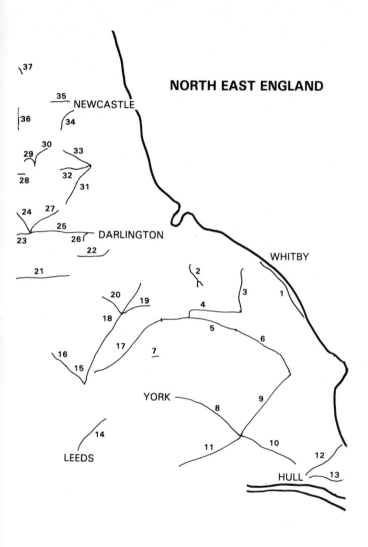

NORTH EAST ENGLAND

NEWCASTLE

DARLINGTON

WHITBY

YORK

LEEDS

HULL

Edinburgh railway line between Darlington and Selby.

III Durham
The whole of County Durham

IV Northumberland
The whole of Northumberland.

The railways were born in the North East; and the reasons were primarily economic. In the 1830's and 1840's expanding industries, mines and mills needed a new transport system to augment the canals and the roads which could no longer cope with their growing orders. Railways, using advance stream technology which enabled them to offer cheap conveyance of bulky, low value goods, were the answer; and as the railway companies developed their passenger sides canal packet boats and stage coaches vanished.

Increased leisure time and more cash combined with cheap, quick travel helped the development of tourism. Hikers with knapsacks could alight at one station, spend the day striding through the countryside and return home from a station miles away from where they had set off. In this way a new breed of rambler came into being.

They came from all levels of society and were, for the most part, enlightened beings to whom class meant little. Their sole purpose in embarking upon these hiking excursions was to forget the humdrum workaday world; to exchange it for a few magical hours in congenial surroundings among people with similar interests. Without railways such pleasures were beyond the reach of most people.

The railways continued to be a major and unchallenged form of transport for goods and passengers until the first World War. It was not until the inter war years that real competition in the shape of the motor car threatened the railway's monopoly. With cars now being assembled on production lines from mass produced components, for the first time they were cheap, fairly reliable and easy to maintain. This conflict between rail and road transport came to a temporary halt during the 1939-45 war as car factories were switched to war production.

With the return of peace, the battle for traffic between rail and road was renewed. Once again cars were mass produced. Petrol was cheap, the roads reasonably traffic free and people were finding that motoring was fun. As more and more cheap cars took to the roads, trains emptied.

On 1st January, 1948, Britain's railways were nationalised.

By 1960 it was clear that something had to be done for the ailing railways.

In 1963 the Beeching Report was published. It recommended that many of the smaller or less profitable branch lines be closed and that duplication routes were to be phased out.

Britain's rail mileage was dramatically reduced from 17,500 in 1962 to 12,400 in 1968. Today less than 11,000 miles of track remain and the shrinkage continues. The motor car has deposed the railway as the premier means of travelling short and even long distances.

Today long lengths of defunct lines are privately owned. Other lines remain open to the public for leisure activities like horse riding and walking. To the railway enthusiast these railway walkways are hallowed for they evoke those halcyon days when steam was king and the rhythmic click clack of bogie wheels stirred the heart and made the adrenalin flow.

By their very nature abandoned railways make for easy walking. Usually no incline is beyond the capability of an engine pulling carriages or rolling stock. For the most part any change of gradient is not too severe; so a reasonably fit walker should encounter few problems in this respect.

Most of the problems associated with walking abandoned lines stem from right of access. Many of these disused old railways, or parts of them, have been divided into sections of various lengths and sold to private buyers. For this reason the would be walker is frequently required to gain permission prior to setting off: but in practice this is seldom refused.

The courteous walker will seldom, if ever, meet serious objections from the people who own that part of the line along which he or she wishes to walk. It is the few thoughtless ones who become involved with self-inflicted difficulties and make things awkward for everyone else. A stroppy approach to a bloody-minded farmer can only lead to a nasty confrontation. A common sense approach, on the other hand, is a winner every time.

Disused lines have a lot to offer the discerning rambler should his or her interest be the local flora and fauna, railway architecture, historical associations or whatever. The variety is infinite. Abandoned railway lines like abandoned spinsters, ache to be loved, thrive on companionship and repay attention in plenty. So beware, innocent would-be-railway rambler, for these disused tracks have infinite

11

Contrasts in locomotive preservation at Grosmont Station NYMR

charm and will interest, enchant and very likely ensnare the unsuspecting with impunity. Should this happen to you - and it probably will - it is best not to resist: for although the magic is long lasting and the addiction difficult to break, I have yet to meet a railway rambler who, smitten with the disease, wants to break the spell. Therefore go to it, throw your inhibitions to the winds, put your best foot forward, explore these disused north eastern railways and have a lot of fun.

KEY TO MAPS

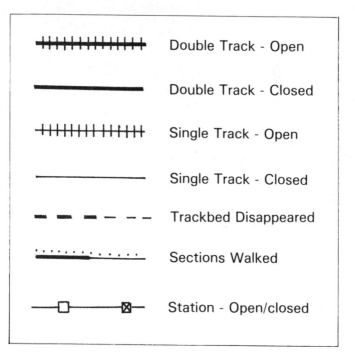

Notes on Maps

To draw a map for every walk in this book would have required a separate book of maps. It was, therfore, necessary to edit these in some way and I have limited the maps to those lines with a more than usual number of railway features and to those where detours are needed.

The maps are only intended to be used as guides and it is recommended that they be read in conjunction with a detailed map such as the 1" or 1:50,000 Ordnance Survey maps.

David Bell

I. North Yorkshire and North Humberside

In fine weather the White Horse of Kilburn can be seen quite clearly from trains speeding up and down the spacious Vale of Mowbray, south of Northallerton. During their journeys along this premier eastern rail link with Scotland, proud expresses, hurrying through the flat, fertile, Yorkshire landscape, skirt old fashioned towns like Thirsk and even older places like the site of the Battle of the Standard. They flash past many picturesque villages in their rush towards distant destinations.

Of those passengers who, not too drowsy with travel, view the passing parade through the carriage windows, most are fully aware that what they are looking at is a slice of Yorkshire. Yet when asked what they consider to be their most evocative Yorkshire scene most will name the North Yorks Moors, that long line of moorland bounding the eastern side of the Vale of Mowbray and on the slope of which the White Horse lies.

The North York Moors, today a vast National Park which, in autumn is ablaze with purple heather, are not as lofty as the Pennines. Yet they exude a mystical air of far reaching solitudes. All the elements of the moorland scene are there: undulating roads, many unfenced, grazing sheep, rough grazing, rough moors rolling away to high wide horizons, and, pushing into them, gentle well formed dales.

Roseberry Topping, the most conspicuous but not the highest hill on the North York Moors, towering above Newton-under-Roseberry as it does, gives them an added sense of the dramatic. In contrast, the peaceful Esk, Cleveland's principal river rises in a desolate moorland hollow at the head of Westerdale and flows eastwards to enter the sea at Whitby where, high above the harbour stand the remains of the famous Abbey of St.Hilda. A superb moorland road climbs out of the lovely Esk valley at Sleights. It runs above the hollow sheltering Goathland, glimpses the curving depths of the Hole of Horcum and edges narrow Newton Dale before descending to the Vale of Pickering.

Thornton-le-Dale, which claims to be the prettiest of Yorkshire villages is one of many lovely hamlets in this delightful vale lying lush and green between the moors and the wolds.

Coastwise south from Whitby the quaint houses of Robin Hoods

Bay huddle together, looking as though they would topple into the sea. Moors separate Robin Hoods Bay from Scarborough, Queen of the Yorkshire Coast, with its two bays separated by a rocky headland with a castle perched on top. A little further on comes Filey with its brig of natural rock forming a pier. Bempton cliffs soar above Filey bay close to Flamborough Head, the most famous promontory on the east coast. Bridlington, which lies in the curving bay south of Flamborough was an historic town long before it became a seaside resort. A third of the way between Brid, as the locals call it, and Spurn Head, at the mouth of the river Humber, lies Hornsea, one time fishing village turned sea-side resort.

North Humberside, which spreads out like a half open fan radiating from Spurn Head, crosses the Wolds and prescribes an arc westwards from Filey. This region, enlarged to include land up to and including York, used to be called the East Riding. It was the smallest of Yorkshire's three Ridings and had York as its capital. It is a little known, thinly populated area despite having been settled longer than any other part of Yorkshire.

North Humberside has little in common with North Yorkshire's moors and dales. Even its coastline is vastly different from that north of Scarborough. At its highest point, at Garrowby Hill, North Humberside just manages to top 800 feet, and all its contours are gentle, the characteristic landscape of chalk and clay. It is a land of dry uplands and sluggish, winding rivers.

The Wolds are home to hundreds of sheep who have occupied the narrow valleys for centuries; and neolithic barrows are scattered about them, one of the largest being at Duggleby Howe.

Some of the finest churches in England are to be found in what was once the East Riding, among them York Minster, Beverley Minster, Bridlington Priory, Hemingborough and Partington and Hedon and Howden, all gloriously English gothic.

Railways are not the only things to have been abandoned in this district: many villages have suffered the same fate.

So vast are the topographical differences between North Yorkshire and what was once the East Riding, so diverse are their interesting features, that anyone seeking variety would be well advised to sample both areas. One of the most rewarding ways of doing so is by walking the disused railways detailed in this part of the book. By so doing you will become deeply involved in the rich, colourful pageant of English history. Start where fancy takes you: but for the purist, the gateway is York.

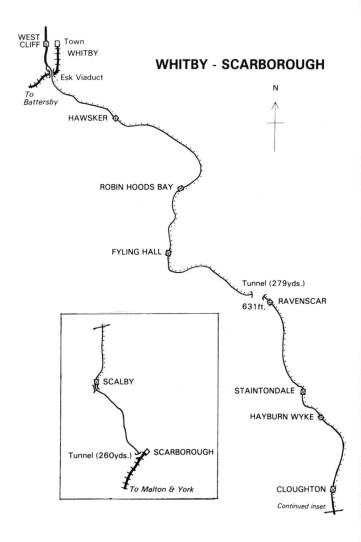

WHITBY - SCARBOROUGH

WEST CLIFF

Town
WHITBY

Esk Viaduct

To Battersby

N

HAWSKER

ROBIN HOODS BAY

FYLING HALL

Tunnel (279yds.)

631ft. RAVENSCAR

SCALBY

STAINTONDALE

HAYBURN WYKE

Tunnel (260yds.) SCARBOROUGH

To Malton & York

CLOUGHTON

Continued inset

1. THE SCARBOROUGH TO WHITBY LINE

Length : 21¾ miles
Opened : 16th July, 1885
Closed : 8th March, 1965
O/S : 1:63,360 - North Yorks Moors tourist map

> *Hurray for the mighty engine:*
> *As he bounds along his track.*
> *Hurray for the life that is in him:*
> *And his breath so thick and black.*
> *Alexander Anderson.*

The Scarborough-Whitby line was built under the auspices of the independent Scarborough and Whitby Railway Company. This company built the intermediate stations and considered building its own termini. However, this idea was abandoned and it was decided that the line should join the N.E.R. at both ends. This led to the building at Scarborough of the 260 yards long Falsgrave tunnel and, at Whitby, the 915 feet long Larpool viaduct over the Esk.

Scalby, the first station North of Scarborough, makes a good starting point the very pleasant scenic walk along the uprooted railway to Whitby, which follows a route roughly parallel and close to the coastal section of the celebrated Cleveland Way long distance walk.

The first part of the walk, to just north of Cloughton station, now a school study centre, is fairly level going. Then the climbing begins, gently at first but becoming steeper just south of Stainton Dale

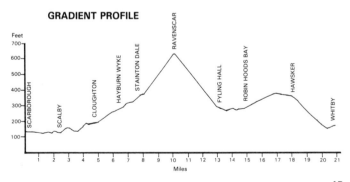

GRADIENT PROFILE

where, for a short stretch, the gradient is 1 in 54. Stainton Dale station is now an agricultural depot managed by the last station master's son.

A ¾ mile diversion to the coast from where a bridge crosses the track half a mile north of Cloughton station is most rewarding. For there, at Cloughton Wyke, well-bedded brown sandstones interspersed with blue-grey clays and silts make the bay very attractive and are a magnet for geologists and photographers. The fishing thereabouts from rocky platforms below the east cliffs is excellent, particularly in the mackerel season.

Shortly beyond Stainton Dale station the way climbs steeply for two miles, to Ravenscar station, at 631 feet above sea level the highest point on the line. The average gradient throughout these two miles is 1 in 41, a hard haul for the steam trains which ran along the line until 1958. The steam drawn scenic excursions which continued to run until 1963 were normally double headed, pulling a maximum of eight bogies and, since they ran in the Whitby to Scarborough direction only they were spared that 1 in 41 climb. However, on the last day of the line an enthusiast's special, headed by two 2-6-0's, did the run from Scarborough to Whitby, which made the firemen sweat more than somewhat.

At the turn of the century the Peak Estate Co. Ltd. hoped to develop 750 acres at Ravenscar into a new seaside resort. The row of shops adjacent to the station and the broad, unmade road leading to it were to be the nucleus of an estate planned for the area. But lack of access to the beach, the cold, north east winds and damp sea fogs discouraged prospective purchasers and the venture collapsed. Today Ravenscar station is derelict.

When the line was in use there used to be a gradient post at the northern end of Ravenscar platform. The arm indicating the stretch on which the station stood was lettered 1 in 1571: the other arm gave the gradient as 1 in 39. So as a train left the station, going north, the change in the inclination of the coaches could be seen quite clearly.

The line offers many superb views of the North Sea, by far the most spectacular being the panoramic sweep of Robin Hood's Bay, spread out some 500 feet below, as seen on emerging from Ravenscar tunnel, walking northwards. It is breathtaking.

Ravenscar tunnel is 279 yards long and is situated near the summit of the aforementioned 1 in 39 gradient just outside Ravenscar station on the Whitby side.

For three gently curving, downhill miles the gradient remains 1 in

River Esk at Whitby

39, then it eases to 1 in 103 and, a quarter of a mile further on the site of Fylinghall station is passed on a 1 in 288 gradient.

A dreaming blend of land and seascapes viewed through a heat haze that seemed to lay a golden sheen over everything, with the soft luminosity of a Turner painting, made our descent from Ravenscar to Robin Hood's Bay one of those happy occasions man records for his mental posterity. Even the old line along which we walked was seductive in its peaceful meanderings. Small wonder that in the days before the track was removed many passengers descended on Robin Hood's Bay, with their heads stuck out of the carriage windows.

Little more than gravity was required to carry a train from Ravenscar station down that 3 miles long 1 in 39 gradient. But travelling in the opposite direction frequently caused problems for Scarborough bound trains because of the steepness of the climb to Ravenscar station. Usually with a capable engine and good, dry conditions the gradient caused no problems. But under wet, greasy conditions many an engine hauling a full load of five carriages got stuck within sight of Ravenscar station.

Robin Hood's Bay station was the most important intermediate station on the line. It had up and down platforms, a signal box, a goods yard and a goods shed. It served a rather special place so when you have inspected what is left of it, have a look at The Bay. You will not be disappointed.

Robin Hood's Bay, once an obscure village and a reputed haunt of smugglers is today a show place for tourists. The coast thereabouts is rich in fossils and geologically interesting. It is a jumble of red roofed buildings built one above another and its labyrinth of passages and steps attract a great deal of attention.

Leaving Robin Hood's Bay station the track begins to climb a steep, 1 in 43, gradient to the clifftops on the north side of the bay. Then, midway between Robin Hood's Bay and Hawsker it descends almost as steeply to cross the river Esk on a fine brick viaduct about a mile upstream from Whitby. The viaduct is 915 feet long, 120 feet high and has 13 arches.

After the viaduct has crossed the River Esk it crosses the Whitby and Pickering line and the Whitby, Redcar and Middlesbrough Union line. This latter line climbs a 1 in 52 gradient from Whitby Town to Westcliff and in doing so comes alongside the line to Scarborough at Prospect Hill junction. It was there that the Scarborough-Whitby line terminated.

Flowers flourish in abundant variety in the clay soils along the track, in particular at Hayburn Wyke. In season the following flowers can be seen along the Scarborough-Whitby line: primrose, bluebell, harebell, clover, vetch, cowslip, wild thyme, small scabious, salad burnet and spotted orchids among others, some quite rare.

Where once the shrill whistles of the engines using the line rent the coastal air, now cries of land birds like lark and peewits blend with those of seabirds like the herring gull and the black headed gull.

Where once trains chuffed along bright rails, now booted feet trudge along a clinkered track.

Looking up Rosedale from Old Kilns. The course of the line can just be seen on the ledge running right round the hillside

2. THE ROSEDALE RAILWAY

Length : 14¼ miles
Opened : To Bank Top - 17th March, 1861
To East Mines - 18th August, 1865
Closed : 13th June, 1929 Goods only - no passenger traffic
O/S : 1:63,360 - North Yorks Moors tourist map

> *In eighteen hundred and sixty one,*
> *I put me cord'roy breeches on.*
> *I put me cord'roy breeches on*
> *To work upon the railway.*
> Anonymous.

What a superb enterprise the Rosedale railway is! Within three miles of leaving its northern terminus, Battersby, the line leaps dramatically from the fertile plain of Cleveland to the peat moors on the roof of the North York moors. There it remains for eleven looping miles, never once dropping below the 1,000 feet contour. The drama is maintained to its southern terminus, Bank Top, where it ends abruptly close to where the moor takes a one in three plunge into Rosedale valley.

21

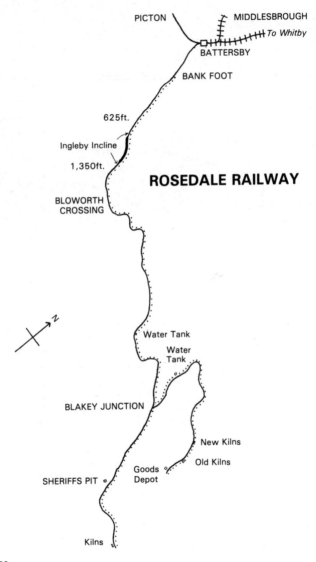

New Kilns - East Rosedale

The line was built to convey iron ore from the Rosedale West Mines via Stokesley to Stockton and Ferryhill. Prior to its creation the ore was hauled by horse and cart to Pickering Station, a difficult operation because part of the route was a 'complete bog from end to end, full of holes two feet deep' with the rest being even worse.

With the exception of the first mile from Battersby to Bank Foot, which is through private land, the whole route is a public right of way. So let's be adventurous and explore this unusual line. To reach our start we have to first take the Ingleby Greenhow to Battersby road going north east from the village, then the first right leading to Bank Foot where a signpost points south along the route of the disused Rosedale line.

For two miles the line hugs the foot of a steep escarpment like the hem of a skirt. Conifers sweeping down from the heights stop abruptly at the line. The trees on our right are deciduous and without the unnatural serried look of their man-planted cousins on the other side of the track.

Beneath the oaks, the elders and the hawthorns, in shady hollows and on sunny banks primrose, violets and wood anemonies grow in their season. Pretty summer flowers bring delight to the lush pastural

23

landscape of the Cleveland Plain, stretching seemingly to infinity. Robins and thrushes, blackbirds and chaffinches build their neat nests and raise their young in the hedges which stitch these irregular fields.

Just beyond an isolated row of inhabited railway cottages the line does a smart left turn to face the escarpment and make a direct assault on it. For almost a mile the line climbs the incline beginning on a gradient of one in eleven which soon becomes one in eight and eventually reaches one in five. The incline looks for all the world like a ski slope, particularly when snow covered. In climbing it we turn our backs on a well husbanded world of mixed farming and face a wild, inhospitable yet exhilarating landscape of peat moors.

Because of its steepness and the sharp angles at the top and bottom of the incline, engines were unable to operate on it. Normally five 0-6-0 tender engines were used above the incline and they were housed at Bank Top, Rosedale. Whenever one needed to be lowered for major repairs the central pair of its three sets of wheels had to be removed. The engine was then hauled eleven miles to the incline top where, without its central wheels, it could be manoeuvred over the sharp angles at both ends of the slope.

Wagons were hauled up the incline by steel ropes, 1650 yards long, which passed around 14 feet diameter drums. The descending loaded wagons, usually three at a time, drew up a set of empty wagons at a speed of 10 m.p.h. The journey usually took three minutes.

At the top of the incline with its magnificent views of the Cleveland Plain there were sidings and some railway buildings, including the drum house, workshops and four cottages known as 'Siberia'.

From the incline top on Greenhow Moor the line remains on the high moors throughout its length, now passing through cuttings, now being carried along embankments around the heads of valleys, always assiduously avoiding their steep sides.

Bloworth Crossing lies a mile beyond the incline top on Rudland Rigg, close to the highest point of the North York Moors. Once two cottages stood there but today only the rough road remains, crossing the line en route to Stokesley from Kirkby Moorside.

The next four miles from Bloworth Crossing to the Esklets become part of the well known Lyke Wake Walk, a 40 miles tramp across the North York Moors. The going is easy along a line that pushes eastwards in two great loops around the head of Farndale.

Farndale, from the Gaelic *'fearna'* meaning the place where alder trees grow, is by far the best known valley of the North York Moors.

*Ruin at East Rosedale. The New Kilns are on the left
and the Old Kilns can be seen through
the window arch*

Springtime is the time to go there when it is ablaze with thousands upon thousands of daffodils that bloom from almost one end of the dale to the other.

Beyond the Farndale loops the line, now going S.E., crosses the Esklets col on a long, straight causeway. It then curves to southwards and begins a mile long climb along the top of the High Blakey Moor escarpment. Within a quarter of a mile of leaving the causeway, close to the eight mile post, stand the remains of a brick built water tower. Close by is the spring fed reservoir which supplied the water. After a further great northwards curve to avoid the crags of Blakey Gill the line arrives at Blakey Junction.

Farndale's daffodils never encroach on the wild, moorland section of the line. The flowers of the hedgerows, which grow in profusion on the Cleveland Plain, refuse to climb the incline. There are no trees on the moor: only great, empty, gale bent tracts of coarse grasses and heather. Therefore blackbirds, thrushes and other hedge nest builders avoid what is for them a hostile environment. But what is alien to one is home to another. Ground nesting birds like skylarks, curlews and grouse thrive on the moors and many make their homes close to the

25

line. It is not unusual to see agitated grouse soar from almost underfoot, land some distance away and, harshly crying 'Go back: go back', watch until the intruder has passed. The curlews 'liquid pipe', often distantly heard, seems to encapsulate the moor's brooding enigma.

The line is always open to the moor. There never were any fences although sheep were everpresent throughout the line's life. It was deemed cheaper to pay for any that were killed accidentally through straying onto the line than to fence the moorland section.

Since the line was, for the most part, single track, signal boxes were not required. Instead, a simple staff system was used with the control point at Blakey Junction, which proved adequate. There was, however, a telephone line along the entire route but this was frequently brought down by snow and gales.

The only bridge along the whole route was at Blakey Junction. It carried the Castleton to Hutton-le-Hole road over the line at a cutting, which was a notorious snow trap. During road improvements in 1954 the bridge arch was filled in but the parapet remains.

Blakey Junction offers a choice of routes. One, the continuation of the Rosedale branch proper, extends in a south easterly direction along the western edge of Rosedale on a gradually falling gradient for over four miles to Bank Top terminus just short of where the Hutton-le-Hole to Rosedale Abbey road plunges so dramatically into the dale bottom.

The other branches northwards towards the head of Rosedale, passing within 300 yards of the Lion Inn, an isolated public house sitting on the 1293ft. contour. A mile from the junction are the ruins of a brick structure that once supported a water tank fed by a nearby reservoir. As the line rounds the head of Rosedale much evidence of the engineering work involved in building it can be seen: extensive cuttings, embankments and buttressing. Having rounded the dale head, the line continues in a southwesterly direction, curling spectacularly around Nab Scar to reach, after four and a half miles from Blakey Junction, its terminus at Low Baring.

The views from both east and west sides of Rosedale, as seen from the line, are spectacular and make a fitting climax to an excellent walk along what, in its heyday, was a most unusual branch line.

3. THE NORTH YORKSHIRE MOORS RAILWAY
The Newtondale Trail

Length :   18 miles
Opened :   1836. As a horse-tramway
              1846. Steam trains introduced
Closed :   1965
              1975 May. Reopened as the N.Y.M.R.
O/S   :   1:63,360 - North Yorks Moors tourist map

> *This train is bound for glory, this train,*
> *This train is bound for glory, this train,*
> *This train is bound for glory,*
> *If you ride in it, you must be holy, this train.*
> *Anonymous.*

When in 1836 the Whitby-Pickering line was opened 'every part of the line where the public could have access to it or where a view of the railway could be obtained, was crowded with spectators'. At Pickering, where 7,000 people turned out, seven bands played and bystanders and those in coaches alike cheered and waved flags.

The route, which had been surveyed by George Stephenson, fresh from his successes with the Stockton and Darlington Railway and the Liverpool-Manchester Railway, quickly became noted for its grandeur; and with good reason. For the brooding, wild landscape of bracken, crags and towering cliffs through which it passes holds the eye with its splendour; and nowhere more so than in Newton Dale gorge.

Once the dale contained a few lonely farm houses but today afforestation dominates.

Approaching Newton Dale gorge from the north the line at Ellerbeck is overlooked by the three famous 'golf balls' of Fylingdales Early Warning System.

The line was built primarily for the transportation of goods and minerals, including Grosmont ironstone and Esk Valley Whinstone, some of which was used in the building of Somerset House and Waterloo Bridge.

A feature of the original line was its exceptionally sharp curves. So severe were they that in 1864 special locomotives, Whitby bogies, were built to cope with them. Their two pairs of bogie wheels were set well back under the boiler and placed closer together than usual.

27

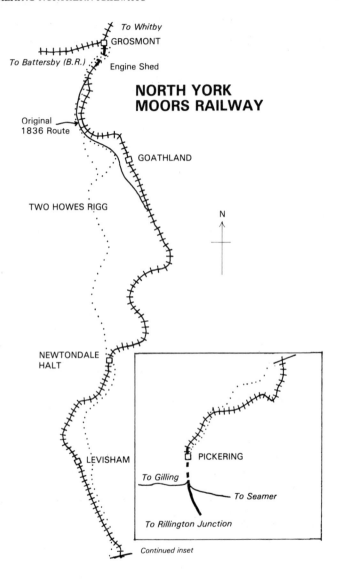

To Whitby

GROSMONT

To Battersby (B.R.)

Engine Shed

NORTH YORK MOORS RAILWAY

Original
1836 Route

GOATHLAND

TWO HOWES RIGG

N

NEWTONDALE
HALT

LEVISHAM

PICKERING

To Gilling

To Seamer

To Rillington Junction

Continued inset

Special coaches with four wheels instead of six were developed for use on the line. They were nicknamed Whitby Bathing Machines. Stephenson had engineered the line with only the horse in mind. Not until steam locomotives were introduced were the curves found to be too severe for normal stock, hence Whitby bogies and special coaches.

The original stable block can still be seen at Grosmont station and the narrow, castellated tunnel there which leads to today's engine shed was once used by horse drawn trains. In Newton Dale there is a house, the Grange, which used to be the Raindale Inn, a changing post for the horses.

Between Grosmont and Goathland, at the lovely village of Beck Hole, there used to be a 500 yards long incline at the foot of which the horse drawn carriages were uncoupled to be hauled up by cable. Charles Dickens, who travelled on the line in 1844 to attend a friend's funeral in Malton, described it as 'a quaint old railway along part of which passengers are hauled by rope'. Steam trains were introduced in 1846 but the hauling of carriages up the incline continued until 1865, when a four mile deviation was opened. Today the incline forms part of the original line and is available to walkers.

It was on the Whitby-Pickering line that the first ever Cheap Day excursion ticket was issued. In 1839 a fête was held at Grosmont to raise money for a new Anglican church. For passengers travelling from Whitby to Grosmont the return fare was reduced from 9d. to 6d. Similar reductions were made for passengers travelling from Pickering and intermediate stations.

George Hudson, the Railway King, introduced steam to the line and improved the track. He acquired the Whitby-Pickering Railway in 1845 and linked it, for the first time to the wider railway network. Thus Hudson became responsible for the development of Whitby as a resort.

In 1965 the Beeching axe fell on the eighteen miles section of the Whitby-Pickering line from Grosmont to Pickering, the remaining six miles from Grosmont to Whitby escaping closure. This six miles long section is still used today by trains operating British Rail's Esk Valley service, a line renowned for the beauty of the countryside through which it runs. Many people see the Esk Valley line as the most beautiful train ride in England.

For two years the defunct Grosmont-Pickering line lay neglected; but not entirely forgotten. In 1967 a remarkable local man, Tom Salmon of Ruswarp, decided that this famous line should not remain neglected and decaying. Together with a handful of supporters, including many railwaymen and ex-railwaymen, he formed a pilot group dedicated to bringing it back to life. So successful were these 'crackpots', as they were at first derided, that in May 1973, the line was re-opened as the North Yorkshire Moors Railway, the Duchess of Kent performing the ceremony.

So many joyous sightseers were at Grosmont to see the Duchess board the ceremonial train to Pickering that they almost blocked the line.

Today the North Yorkshire Moors Railway is one of Yorkshire's most popular attractions.

A superb 20 miles long walk, the Newtondale Trail, devised by Mike Teanby of Doncaster, links the terminal stations of the N.Y.M.R. The railway forms an integral part of the trail by providing a focal point throughout the walk. The detailed route directions, which follow, are for those walking from Pickering to Grosmont; but the walk can be done equally well in the other direction. The return journey to base is by train - steam or diesel - at the end of the day.

The Route

From Pickering station follow a minor road to cross the railway at Newbridge and turn right along a tarmac track to Park Gate. Turn left at the gate beyond the house to ascend the bankside on a green track and follow through to Blansby Park top farm. Pass through farm gates and head N.N.E. across a grass field to a gate in the far corner and continue on a track alongside cultivated fields to a derelict building. Keeping to your original bearing, cross a fence and pass to the right of a building and cross a field to enter a plantation through a gate in the far corner. Continue on a forest track for 300 yards and turn right at a junction of tracks for a further 200 yards, then right again to leave the track at a slight bend and follow an indistinct path downhill to Farwath. Cross Pickering Beck over a footbridge and the railway and turn left through a handgate to follow an intermittent path through fields and woodland adjacent to the railway for 1¼ miles. At the handgate (Waymark) in the boundary fence, follow a good track uphill through a plantation onto a level grass track leading to the Levisham road. Follow the road downhill to a left-hand bend half a mile from the station and continue directly ahead on a wide level grass track to Skelton Tower. Turn right at the tower and contour around the edge of the moor on a narrow path to Yew Tree Scar above Talbotwood. Keeping to the right of a stream turn left off the moor top and descend steeply on a good path with stiles to Newtondale.

In the dale bottom cross the stream over a footbridge and turn left at a sign to follow a path alongside the stream and through the railway underpass into Newtondale Halt. Here, if need be, you can catch a train for Pickering or Grosmont.

Directly opposite the railway turn left along a forest track for 200 yards and find and turn right along an indistinct path to climb steeply to an upper track. Then turn left through a wood to emerge at a sharp bend of the main forest drive. Continue along the drive and turn right at the second fire break, then turn left along an adjoining wide fire break through the plantation to a gate in the boundary fence. Turn right alongside a fence to pass a derelict building at Wardle Green and go out onto the open moorland. Keeping to the moor top, cross a pathless section of rough heather to join and follow a good path with cairns from Simon Howe triangulation pillar over Two Howes Rigg down to the roadside near the Mallyan Spout Hotel in Goathland. Turn left down a signed path to the right of the hotel and descend to West Beck. Mallyan Spout is nearby on the left (off route) but the trail turning right, follows a well walked beckside footpath with signs and stiles to Grosmont station.

Grid References
The following grid reference may be useful:-
Pickering (799842) Blansby Park (825867) Farwath (829883) Yew Tree Scar (838976) Newtondale Halt (834948) Wardle Green (824963) Simon Howe (830881) Mallyan Spout (824010) Grosmont (828053)

Trains
A scheduled service runs between Pickering and Grosmont from Easter until the end of October. Timetables are available from the Ticket Office, N.Y.M.R. Pickering, North Yorkshire.

Trail Award
No time limit is imposed for the completion of the Newtondale Trail although an experienced walker would aim to complete it as a single day expedition in about 7 hours.

For those completing the walk, rucsac badges are available from **Mike** Teanby, 60, High Street, Norton, Doncaster, Yorkshire.

Anyone wishing to tackle a railway walk that is somewhat **different will find** this one has all the required ingredients.

4. THE PICKERING-GILLING-.PILMOOR LINE

Length :   44 miles
Opened :   Pilmoor to Gilling - 19th May, 1853
            Gilling to Helmsley - 9th October, 1871
            Helmsley to Kirkby Moorside - 1st January, 1874
            Kirkby Moorside to Pickering - 1st April, 1875
Closed :   Kirkby Moorside to Pickering - 2nd February, 1953
            Gilling to Kirkby Moorside
            To Passenger traffic - 2nd February 1953
            To goods traffic - August 1964
            Pilmoor to Gilling - March, 1963
O/S   :   Sheets 99 & 100 - Scale 1:50,000

> *We flash across the level,*
> *We thunder thro' the bridges,*
> *We bicker down the cuttings,*
> *We sway along the ridges.*
> *W.E.Henley. 1849-1903*

Pilmoor station, which today is deserted and derelict came into being in 1847 when, on 17th June of that year, a branch line from Boroughbridge to Pilmoor was opened with the sole object of serving the Boroughbridge district by making connections with main line trains.

Pilmoor station was a place apart, there being no road access to it and no village to serve.

During the years 1865-6 as part of a scheme to make a route from Leeds to Scarborough without passing through York, the Great North of England Company inserted a link between Boroughbridge to Pilmoor and the Pilmoor to Malton lines a short distance to the south of Pilmoor station. Embankments and a bridge over the main line were built and track was laid. But, in the interests of economy, the plan was dropped.

At the Malton end of the line the curve onto the Scarborough line was not even begun.

The rails along the link were removed in 1885 and the bridge over the main line demolished in 1932.

The line from Gilmoor to Pilling cuts through a broad, rich agricultural area of neatly patterned fields. It all looks so natural yet it is a man made landscape created by enclosures made largely in the 100

Helmsley Parish Church on a sunny afternoon in late autumn

years between 1750 and 1850 to exploit new methods of farming. They arrived before the railways, but only just. For between 1845 and 1855 almost 5000 miles of track, including the line from Pilmoor to Gilling, were constructed throughout the land.

Of all the Yorkshire branch lines growing from Joseph Pease's Great North of England Railway's main line, the one from Pilmoor eastwards was very likely the most rural. Throughout its journey to Gilling it takes advantage of the flat, rural landscape, passing between the Hambleton and the Howardian hills through the Coxwold-Gilling gap.

To northwards from the long embankment which runs most of the way from Husthwaite to Coxwold there are fine views of the 314 feet long White Horse of Kilburn. It looks impressive but is a fairly new feature having been cut out by a local schoolmaster in 1857. His pupils marked the outline and 30 local men did the rest.

Although the White Horse holds no claim to antiquity, Husthwaite does. As its name implies, the village is of Saxon origin. 'Hus' is the Saxon word to 'house' and 'thwaite' is the Norse for 'clearing'.

An unusual feature of the place is that its houses are made of mellow, weathered brickwork, unlike other surrounding villages which, for the most part, are built of local, pale stone. Then there is its

Tudor cottage, overlooking the village green. In the north these are almost as rare as hen's teeth.

There is a pub in Coxwold called 'The Fauconberg Arms'. It is named after Earl Fauconberg of Newburgh Priory, south east of the village. His wife, Mary, was Oliver Cromwell's daughter and she is said to have brought his body to the priory after the Restoration of Charles II in 1660. There it was buried in a brick vault which has never been opened.

Eastward bound trains to both Pickering and Malton were routed onto their respective lines at Gilling. For two miles these lines run parallel, then the Pickering line swung north to cross the River Rye and keep it company to Helmsley. This routing procedure was instituted to save the expense of making a physical junction and therefore a signal box where the tracks diverged

The River Rye, south of Helmsley, flows gently through broad, well husbanded acres laced with footpaths and narrow country roads. It is a green and pleasant land and the route of the old railway is wick with wildlife.

At Helmsley rail route and River Rye part company, the former making a great loop to eastwards via Helmsley station which is at the south east corner of this most attractive Yorkshire Market town.

Helmsley, which today is rapidly developing into an important tourist centre and which is the administrative centre of the North York Moors National Park, has its roots in the distant past. In the twelfth century, Rubert de' Roos, Lord of Helmsley, began to fortify the place. In 1644 Parliamentary forces led by Sir Thomas Fairfax of Gilling laid siege to Helmsley Castle. Royalist forces under Colonel Crossland held out for three months before surrendering. Parliament then ordered the castle to be dismantled; but sufficient remains, in particular the ruinous Keep, to show the original fortifications.

The chimes of Helmsley parish church, All Saints, have to be heard to be believed. They strike four times every quarter hour and 27 times on the hour. Added to this lot are the hourly strokes so that at midday there are 39 chimes from this ding-dong happy timepiece. This used to be repeated at midnight but because so many visitors complained that the chimes kept them awake, the clock is silent between 11 p.m. and 6 a.m.

The cross in Helmsley market square is the start of the long distance moor and coast walk called the Cleveland Way. But the disused railway track eastwards to Pickering offers a dozen equally interest

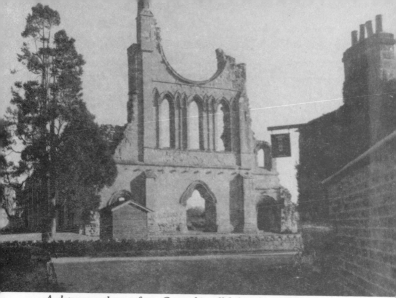

*A detour north-east from Coxwold will bring the walker to
Byland Abbey at the foot of the North Yorkshire Moors*

filled miles along the lower slopes of the tabular, limestone hills where
Bransdale, Farndale and Rosedale enter the Vale of Pickering.

The track skirts the edge of the old glacial lake of Pickering which
some 2,000 years ago, during the Ice Age, was 24 miles long and
between 4 and 6 miles wide. The landscape through which it passes is
a mixture of grass and cereals. Herds of Fresians graze in adjacent
pastures, alongside fields of barley. On its embankment slopes and in
the cuttings foxgloves, thistles, wild roses and brambles grow in
glorious confusion. In common with many other disused lines its
bridges have been demolished; but to the enthusiastic walker of
disused lines this constitutes a challenge.

Several classes of engines including N8 and N9 0-6-2 Ts were used
on this line in the 1930's and by 4-4-0s of classes D17/2, D20 and D49
in the 1940's.

Pickering is a busy market town best seen in springtime when all the
verges are awash with daffodils. It was founded by Perederus, a king
of the Brigantes. William the Conqueror devasted the place during his
harrying of the north. Yet despite this, the Normans gave Pickering a
splendid castle. It is one of the finest examples of a motte and bailey
castle in the north of England.

The White Horse at Kilburn is a landmark visible for many miles around south of Thirsk. It can be seen on our walk from Pilmoor to New Coxwold

Pickering has two Swans, one Black and one White, and in either of them, over a pint, it is nice to reminisce about the places the Pickering-Pilmoor line used to visit. But for those the line would never have been built and we would have been deprived of some excellent walking.

5. THE MALTON-GILLING-PILMOOR LINE

Length : 38¼ miles
Opened : 19th May, 1853
Closed : Malton to Gilling
              To passenger traffic - 1st January, 1931
              To goods traffic - 2nd February, 1953
              Gilling to Pilmoor - March, 1963
O/S : .Sheets 99 and 100 - Scale 1:50,000

> *Among sick varied scenes as these*
> *of hills an' meadows, rocks an' trees,*
> *I live fra trouble free:*
> > Tom Twistleton.

From Pilmoor to two miles east of Gilling the Malton and Pickering lines followed the same route. Then, as the Pickering line took a northerly course to Helmsley and beyond, the Malton line curved gently towards Malton Station on a south-easterly course roughly parallel with and south of the River Rye.

During the summer months, in particular, both during the L.N.E.R. and B.R. days the line was used extensively for passenger trains, bound to and from Scarborough. This relieved congestion at York although the system required the trains to reverse twice at Malton.

Many types of engines were used on these summer services to Scarborough ranging from 0-6-0 classes J21 and J23 to V2 2-6-2s and A1s, A3 and A4 Pacifics.

The track weaves its rural way through a patchwork of green fields. In some Fresians graze, others have sheep while a few are empty Other fields are given over to arable farming. Many contain winter wheat, barley, potatoes and turnips. Evidence of good husbandry abounds. Everything blends: all is harmonious and restful.

Hovingham, eight miles west of Malton, fits its surroundings like a glove. It's stones are tinged with gold, it's roofs ruddy-tiled and, in season, the cottage gardens are a riot of colour. Presiding over this delightful spot is Hovingham Hall, designed in the Mid 18th Century by Sir Thomas Worsley, surveyor general to King George III. There are two hostelries, one a 19th century coaching inn called the Worsley Arms and the other called The Malt Shovel. It is all rather up market, as was Hovingham station. Rail passengers never, ever travelled to Hovingham, for there was no station of that name. It had a much grander appellation. It was called Hovingham Spa.

As it approaches Malton, the line crosses the River Derwent and in so doing moves from the old North Riding to the Old East Riding.

The River Derwent is an odd ball because although it rises on the North York Moors within six miles of the sea, it flows sixty miles before emptying into the Humber and losing its identity; and along its whole length there is only one town, Malton.

Once across the river the way is over the York-Scarborough line - the bridge has long since been demolished - and on to where a link doubles back to the York-Scarborough line close to Malton station.

6. THE MALTON AND DRIFFIELD RAILWAY

Length : 20 miles
Opened : 19th May, 1853
Closed : For passengers traffic - 5th June, 1950
For goods traffic - 20th October, 1958
O/S : Sheets 106 and 107 - Scale 1:50,000

> *Father: What brought thee back lad?*
> *Son: Father! the same feet*
> *As took me brought me back, I warrant ye.*
> *Father: Couldst thou not find the rail?*
> *Son: The deuce himself*
> *Who can find most things, could not find the rail.*
> *W.S.Lander (1775-1864)*

The Malton and Driffield was an independently built railway and its prime job was to serve the chalk quarries at Burdale and Wharram-le-Street. Its construction was something of an engineering triumph for steep gradients and the mile long Burdale tunnel was necessary to lift it out of the Vale of Pickering onto the Wolds. Although, traffic was never very heavy the line proved its worth, especially in winter, to the farmers of the Wolds.

On leaving Malton station, which, unlike Malton town is south of the River Derwent and in the East Riding the line takes a generally southwards direction through gently undulating countryside. But before leaving Norton it runs through land which now belongs to a bacon factory, Porkside Ltd. Thereabouts the air is heavy with the smell of bacon being smoked; and scavenging gulls circle overhead seeking easy pickings.

Three miles south east of Malton the pleasant village of Settrington straddles a tiny beck which rises on the Wolds and makes a large loop southwards before flowing gently northwards and through the village that carries its name.

A Jurassic limestone belt which extends south-westwards across England divides the Vale of Pickering from the Wolds. North Grimston is situated on this belt. It is a lovely place in a richly wooded area. Deciduous trees abound, many being fine sycamores and chestnuts.

As the line threads its way through the Jurassic limestone belt and climbs along a Wolds valley the landscape changes. For the Wolds is a

39

country of porous chalk which does not hold water, so consequently no streams are seen. In fact the scenery resembles more closely the Downs of southern England than it does the moors and dales of the north.

Wharram-le-Street makes an ideal springboard from which to explore Duggleby Howe a couple of miles or so to eastwards. It lies 200 yards south east of Duggleby church, just off the main road, and is one of the largest round barrows ever found in Britain. It is 120 feet in diameter and 20 feet high. Excavations there have unearthed at least 50 cremation remains and the skeletons of many adults and children together with flint arrow heads, beavers' teeth, blades made from boars' teeth and bone skewer pins.

To anyone interested in British history and pre-history the barrows at Duggleby Howe and other Wold sites like Sharp Howes and Willerby Wold are of particular importance for they have survived from the New Stone and Bronze Ages. Because of them we know that there have been Wolds men since Stone Age times.

The sites of many deserted villages can be found in the Wolds close to the course of the Malton and Driffield railway. They date in part from the Black Death in 1349 and in part from the coming of sheep farming in the 15th and 16th centuries. It was not until the 18th century that arable farms began to be enclosed with the result that in many Wold villages only a church dates from an earlier period.

South of Wharram-le-Street but before Burdale Tunnel is reached a branch to the left leads off to Wharram chalk quarry, which was last worked in the 1940's. Its huge stone crusher is still standing but vegetation is gradually covering the old working face. The quarry is now a nature reserve released from the Birdsall Estate Co. Ltd. to the Yorkshire Naturalist Club whose members have free access to it. Unaccompanied non-members require a permit.

Burdale Tunnel lies between the Wharram and Burdale quarries. It has the reputation of being the worst mile along the whole line. Gangers working in it used to say that it was 'murder' because of the black slime that covered everything, the icicles which formed on its roof in winter and the spray the engines threw up on their way through it. Moreover, it 'had a smell of its own'. It still has.

Burdale Quarry, at the southern end of the tunnel, like Wharram, supplied 99% pure chalk to the Redcar steel mills. The chalk left Burdale in train loads of nine wagons which were doubled to eighteen at Wharram.

Burdale station once had a coal depot, sales being the station masters perk. Today only the coal depot siding supports remain. The station buildings are steadily decomposing and the platform is overgrown.

From Burdale Tunnel, the summit of the line, the way is E.S.E., via Garton-on-the-Wolds to Driffield through unspectacular, but satisfying scenery. A.J.Brown, walker extraordinary, wrote in 'Tramping in Yorkshire', 1932. 'There is about the Wold country a quietness and benignity not elsewhere (I think) to be found in the shire'. Winifred Holtby, who was a Woldswoman, has this to say about the Wold country in her novel 'Anderby Wold', 1923 'Fold upon fold of the encircling hills piled rich and golden beneath a tranquil sky'.

Most signs of the Malton and Driffield Railway have now vanished and much is now privately owned so permission must be sought. The dry Wold valley along which it wound its way by Wharram Percy, a deserted medieval village, from North Grimstone to Burdale is melancholy and the Wolds themselves have about them a lovely beauty. It is an area well worth visiting. For as A.J.Brown wrote in 'Yorkshire's Broad Acres', 1948: 'Truly it is in the Wolds that one derives perhaps the best impression of a land of broad acres, for from any of the gentle ridges one looks over immense vistas of undulating arable land, acres and acres of corn and green pastures'.

If there is a better reason than that for walking the route of the old Malton-Driffield Railway I have yet to hear it.

7. THE EASINGWOLD RAILWAY

Length : 2½ miles
Opened : July, 1891
Closed : To passenger traffic November, 1948
         To Goods traffic 28th December, 1957
O/S : Sheet 100 - Scale 1:50,000

Here is a child who clambers and scrambles,
All by himself and gathering brambles;
Robert Louis Stevenson (1850-1894)

It was a lovely little branch running from Easingwold to link with the main East Coast line at Alne and not much of it remains. Easingwold station is a shadow of its former self with little of its past glory remaining. The station buildings were destroyed by fire on 13th June, 1967, and the road wagons shed has gone, but the engine shed still stands.

At the other end of the line, at Alne, there is less to see, most of the station buildings having been demolished. Two years after the closing of the line, during the construction of the up slow line, the Easingwold bay was completely destroyed.

It is the bit in the middle, the 2½ miles long trackbed that is most interesting. It makes a fine vantage point from which to commune with nature. For, in common with other longer, disused lines nature is making an excellent job of obliterating what man has discarded.

In the timetable nature uses, as opposed to that used by mankind, the railway has put in only a brief appearance; and once man lets go, nature quickly sets about removing the traces. All disused railways show this trend. What makes the Easingwold Railway so special is its lack of length. A 2½ mile stretch is long enough to offer a good variety of flora and fauna yet short enough to allow the walker to forget about serious walking for once and concentrate on prodding and poking into the hidden surprises to be found under stones, fallen branches and hedgerows.

Soon after the line was opened the original engine, a Hudswell Clarke 0-4-0 st. was replaced by a six-coupled saddle tank engine called Easingwold. After twelve years this was replaced by a similar engine called Easingwold No. 2. This engine continued in service for 44 years until 1947, by which time it was beyond repair. For the last ten years of the line's life a J71 or J72 0-6-0 T. was hired from British

42

Railway's York shed.

Where once those sturdy engines plied, wildlife is re-establishing itself along the trackbed and the rimming hedgerows. These hedges not only add interest to a walk along a disused line they perform a most important function. For a hedge is a sanctuary for wildlife and when it is lost so is the wildlife it harbours.

The tangles of briers and brambles that encroach on the trackway support a great many animals, particularly insects. These insects provide food for predators, many of which are seed eating birds which catch the insects to supplement their diets.

The hedges along the Easingwold Railway are home to many birds including tits, hedge sparrows, blackbirds, thrushes and chaffinches. In winter, migrants like the fieldfare and the redwing are to be found there, feeding on hips, haws and other berries, and being able to tarry a while and study these birds is one of the delights of walking a very short line like the Easingwold Railway. For with so little walking to do, much time can be devoted to the study of these birds and more.

Easingwold Railway may have died but its ghost remains to make an exciting adventure for nature lovers.

8. THE YORK TO MARKET WEIGHTON LINE

Length   :   20 miles
Opened :   3rd October, 1847
Closed   :   29th November, 1965
O/S   :   Sheet 106 - Scale 1:50,000

> *Come spur away, I have no patience for a longer stay*
> *But must go down and leave the changeable noise of the great town.*
> *I must the country see.*
> *Thomas Randolph*

It was the Manchester and Leeds Railway Company that first prepared a scheme for a branch line from York to Hull via Market Weighton; and it was George Hudson, the railway King, who thwarted their efforts.

Hudson was not an engineer: nor did he know a lot about the workings of a railway. He was, first and foremost a financial manager; and a very successful one despite his dubious business methods. In 1844 he established the Midland Railway Company out of many smaller adjacent companies. Similar amalgamations followed and his financial empire, based on the Midland Railway grew.

When he heard of the Manchester and Leeds Railway Company's scheme, Hudson checked on the proposed route and noticed that it would have to pass through land belonging to the Duke of Devonshire. Acting swiftly, Hudson bought the Duke's home, Londesborough Park, and 12,000 acres for £470,000. It was a deal that made the Nation gasp, it pleased his supporters and alarmed his rivals.

The line, his line, was opened on 3rd October, 1847. On it he had built his own private station half a mile N.W. of the public station at Londesborough. Between his station and his newly acquired stately home, into which he and his wife had moved, he planted a magnificent avenue of trees, two miles long, down which he could be driven. There was a small part of the freshly bought Devonshire estate for which Hudson could find no use. He sold it to his own Company at a profit to himself of £18,000. There you have the measure of the man.

The western end of the line is Bootham Junction where it leaves the York to Scarborough line and curves eastwards to cross the half mile distant River Foss. Bootham Junction is in the York parish of New Earswick on the northern edge of the city. It can be reached along a short path going N.W. from the end of an even shorter street leading right from the B1363 just before it crosses the Scarborough line, going

44

north. From then on the way is straightforward, hedge edged cinder track walking through the parishes of Huntington, Stockton-on-the-Forest, Upper Helmsley and Gate Helmsley. It crosses the River Derwent on a brick viaduct just before reaching Stamford Bridge. Then it is onwards, straight as the flint of an arrow, by Pocklington and Londesborough to Market Weighton.

A couple of years after it had been built someone remarked at one of the N.E.R. half yearly meetings that it was 'a beautifully made line but, unfortunately, without passengers to travel on it'. It was a double line and throughout its life a quiet one. In its later years it gave an outlet from Hull to the north. In the 1960's B.R. decided to make it a single track to save money as traffic had decreased. They also planned to install automatic controlled barriers at many of the level crossings. However, soon after this expensive work had begun, B.R. had a rethink and decided to close the line.

Throughout its length the track lies on a base of red sandstone overlaid with fertile alluvial deposits, first of sand, then clay in the Derwent valley, with more sandstone towards the Wolds. Throughout, the land is difficult to drain.

Some fields adjacent to the line, which are subjected to constant flooding, are kept under permanent grass from which silage is made and beasts fattened. Sometimes some of the fields are left fallow for three years, followed by oats or wheat.

Stamford Bridge is where King Harold defeated the Norse leader, Harold Hardrada, in 1066, only a few days before being defeated himself by William the Conqueror at Hastings.

Pocklington station was 6 yards long and roofed in iron work and glass. The platforms beneath it were covered in weeds and the windows and doors were all broken when, in the late 60s, the recently appointed head of Pocklington school, Guy Willatt, persuaded the Governors of Pocklington school to buy it. Thus the station, the station master's house and four railway cottages became school property for the bargain price of £6,000. During the following three years both platforms were removed, a floor was laid, each end of the station was bricked up and heating and lighting were installed. Today Pocklington school owns one of the most impressive school owned indoor sports centres in the country thanks to the foresight of a remarkable man.

Almost midway between Pocklington and Market Weighton, near the Hamlet of Burnby, a short detour N.E. along a narrow, country road through Nunburnholme will bring you to Warter village. Thereabouts is a setting for the oldest and strangest horse race in England, the Kiplincotes Derby, run every year on the third Thursday in March.

Traditionally the year the race was first run was 1519, the date shown on the winning post by the side of the lane leading from the A163 to Warter; but this is disputed. The first authentic record of the race puts it at 1555 and at that time it was called Kibling Cotes. In 1618 it was founded as the Kiplingcotes Derby and endowed by Lord Burlington and 'five noble men, 19 baronets and 25 gentlemen of the county of Yorkshire'. Between them, these 50 men contributed 360 shillings, the interest from which was the prize money.

The race is open to horses of all ages and they must carry ten stones exclusive to saddle. The weigh-in takes place near the winning post and flints are added and hung around the waist of any underweight rider.

All competitors must enter before 11 o'clock on the morning of the race, which must be run before 2 p.m. It is about four miles long and run, for the most part, along a rough track across fields, ending in a metalled lane near Warter.

The winner receives the interest on the original endowment, about £15 to £20 these days. The second frequently fares much better, receiving £4 out of each entry fee of £4.25. Since there may be a dozen or more entries, he or she can expect to pick up about £40 to £50. The few pounds remaining are used by the Committee to cover any expenses, thus making the Kiplingcotes Derby the most economically run horse race in the land.

George Hudson's private station is no more; and most of the trees along the once fine avenue linking it with his residence have long since vanished. The avenue itself has survived and can best be seen from a minor road between the A163 and Londesborough village.

Londesborough village station is now a memory.

This defunct line, so interesting in itself, provides some good bases from which to visit other closely sited places of interest, so becoming a means to an end as well as an end in itself.

9. THE MARKET WEIGHTON TO DRIFFIELD LINE

Length :	13¾ miles
Opened :	1st May, 1980
Closed :	To goods traffic - 1964
	To passenger traffic - 14th June, 1965
O/S :	Sheets 105 and 106 - Scale 1:50,000

> *Faster than fairies, faster than witches,*
> *Bridges and houses, hedges and ditches;*
> *And charging along like troops in a battle,*
> *All through the meadows, the houses and cattle.*
> *Robert Louis Stevenson*

The wooden fence across the old Driffield line at its junction with the old Beverley line at Market Weighton was not put there to deter would-be-walkers along old railway tracks. It simply divides the private from the publicly owned; and, in fact, the farmer who owns the length of track immediately beyond this fence, along what was the old Driffield line, is only too pleased to allow people to walk along it. His attitude is very enlightened and I am certain that because of it walkers hold him in high esteem and go to great lengths to ensure that they do no damage to his property. Further along the line, however, others take a less helpful attitude, which is a pity. To be on the safe side, anyone wishing to walk along the line from Market Weighton, through the Central Wolds, to Driffield would be well advised to seek permission before setting off.

The Market Weighton to Driffield line was not the first railway to penetrate the Wolds. That distinction goes to the Bridlington to Filey section of the York and North Midland branch from Seamer on the York-Scarborough line. But, during its construction, the long cutting that had to be made through chalk near Enthorpe was as notable as anything the Bridlington to Filey line had to offer.

The line was promoted and built by an independent company although the N.E.R. worked it and in 1914 took it over completely. Traffic from the West Riding to Bridlington and Scarborough could be hauled along it from Selby to Driffield without passing through either York or Hull and this proved extremely valuable.

The Central Wolds landscape through which it passes contrasts greatly with the flat lands across which the York-Market Weighton branch ran. For the Central Wolds are lonely, empty places with gently rounded, often steep sided hills where isolated farms, set back

47

down their own lanes, are surrounded by enclosed fields and sheltered by trees.

On leaving Market Weighton the track goes along an embankment, the sides of which are a tangle of coarse grasses, brambles, shrubs and trees. After about half a mile it bridges the Goodmanham road, and skirts the western flank of Goodmanham village, which is sited in a shallow gap between the Central and Southern Wolds. It is a spring village with an ancient past as shady as its trees and a prominent Norman church reputedly built on the site of a heathen temple.

The Venerable Bede called the village 'this onetime place of idols....called Godmundingham'. This was a reference to an incident that happened there in 627 A.D. when the pagan King Edwin, ruled Northern England. Edwin's chief priest, Corfi, was also a pagan, but another priest, St. Paulinus, was a Christian. It was St. Paulinus who converted the King to Christianity. On the day of his conversion the King and all his court went to 'Godmundingham' and destroyed the pagan temple. Corfi, whom St. Paulinus had also converted was the first to throw his spear against it. When the temple had been destroyed, they all rode to York where they founded York Minster. In this way the north of England began to be converted to Christianity.

The shelter belts and woodlands the disused line passes on its gradual climb onto the Central Wolds were planted by 18th century landowners when they enclosed and developed their estates.

Because the Wold at Enthorpe was too steep sided for a railway to climb, a long, deep, steep sided cutting had to be hacked through the chalk to make the gradient workable; and what an impressive piece of railway it was! I don't suppose it will ever be filled in. Too much air in it!

Once through the cutting, a glorious panorama of rolling uplands unfolds, sweeping back to clear cut horizons. Here sheep graze on the slopes beneath spacious skies, Suffolk cross ewes predominating. This hardy breed is favoured by the Wold's farmers for breeding purposes. Each autumn large numbers of store lambs are brought in from the northern auction marts for fattening up before Christmas, to be replaced by others bought later. It is reckoned that 15-20 lambs can be fattened from one acre of land. The following spring the store lambs are taken away, the land is ploughed and crops, usually barley, are sewn.

Because of increased mechanisation on this and other cereal growing parts of the Wolds, hedges have been grubbed up. The landscape is reverting to its pre-enclosure state with huge fields stretching into the distance. What hedges remain are usually hawthorn with elder in exposed places and willow in low lying areas.

Wending its way across the Central Wolds, the track is verged with grassland that supports a wide range of flowering plants, most of which are common to all the Wolds. Doddery grass, clover, cowslips, sheep's fescue and various vetches all grow there, quite happily, on the chalk; and their presence attracts a great many butterflies, some of which have no other home. Moths, too, are likely to be seen in great numbers because the caterpillars from which they come feed on the leaves of plants endemic to the Wolds; and many of these are to be found growing near this disused railway.

Great numbers of bumble bees buzz about the old four foot, seeking nectar. Many snails, purse spiders, beetles and grass-hoppers spend their lives on and around the chalk railbed. All feel at home there; and non more so than the snails who thrive there because, by means of special glands they form their shells from the chalk.

Once the track has breasted the Central Wold it begins to lose its bird life, simply because there is no surface water. Wheatears, skylarks and meadow pipits can be seen there, but a more rewarding area for the ornithologist is in the woods, below the spring line, where a much greater variety of bird life is to be found.

It does not necessarily follow that because bird life is scarce the same applies to animal life. Moles, hares, hedgehogs, voles and shrews all find the chalk uplands well suited to their requirements. Moles, in particular, love the light soil because it is ideal for tunnelling through and rich in earth worms, their staple diet. Yum! Yum! I suspect that there are more moles burrowing under the Market Weighton-Driffield line than there are in sensitive, Government circles.

All the roads intersecting the track were there long before the line was built, having been created at the time of the enclosures. Between hedges they can be as wide as 60 feet with a central metalled surface. Gypsies make camp sites on these wide verges, farmers plant crops on them and some villages use them as tips. What lovers do on them is anyone's guess.

To people walking along a particular section of the track these intersecting roads make useful entrances or exits. But since the quality of the whole walk is so good, I should think that nothing short of a good downpour would induce anyone to curtail so exhilarating an adventure.

Kiplingcotes Station, Hudson Way. There is also a goods shed
(just visible on left) and a signal box
yet there is no village nearby

10. THE HUDSON WAY
(MARKET WEIGHTON TO BEVERLEY)

Length :   11½ miles
Opened :   1st May, 1865
Closed :   December 1965
O/S   :   Sheet 106 - Scale 1:50,000

> *I know a bank whereon the wild thyme blows,*
> *Where ox-lips and the nodding violet grows;*
> *Quite over-canopied with bush woodline,*
> *With sweet musk roses and with eglantine,*
> *There sleeps Titania.*
> *William Shakespeare*

I know a bank where the dog rose grows where the white clover
spreads and the robin goes. Titania would love it for she would feel at
home there. It is a 1¼ miles long argosy of things natural, a vignette of
the English countryside, stretching eastwards from the site of Market

Weighton railway station along the line to Beverley. Developed as an educational nature reserve, this magical place is an integral part of an enterprising venture undertaken by the Technical Services Department of Humberside County Council.

Following an enlightened policy of purchasing for public use such disused railway lines as become available within their jurisdiction, Humberside County Council bought the complete 11½ miles long defunct Market Weighton to Beverley line, of which the aforementioned nature reserve is an important part. Although much work remains to be done before the conversion is complete, what has been accomplished so far has made other authorities cast envious eyes in the direction of Humberside.

The Yorkshire giant, William Bradley, 7ft. 9inches tall and weighing 27 stones, was a Market Weighton man who died in 1820 aged 33 years, having made a fortune as a fairground freak. It was not surprising, then, that when it came to giving the old Market Weighton to Beverley track a name, that of a railway giant was chosen. The Hudson Way was named after the famous railway promotor George Hudson, even though he had never had any direct association with the Market Weighton to Beverley line.

Son of a yeoman farmer, George Hudson was born in 1800 in a village near York. At 15 he was working as a counter assistant in a draper's shop where he did well, married the daughter of one of the partners and became a partner himself. When he was 27 a great uncle left him a legacy of £30,000 and this enabled him to become an important businessman, moving in the right financial, political and social circles. In 1833, on being told that the railways were coming to York, he became one of the local promoters. The following year, 1834, he met George Stephenson, who fired his imagination with talk of covering the whole countryside with a railway network. In 1839 he opened his first line, the York and North Midland, which he later extended. In 1834 he amalgamated three lines into the Midland Railway. By 1848 he controlled more than a quarter of the U.K. railway network. Put another way, it meant that within 10 years of opening his first railway he had built from scratch a railway empire worth £30 million.

George Hudson became one of England's first millionaires. He was the toast of London, was fêted by the aristocracy and introduced to royalty; for the whole country in the 1840's was railway mad and the railway companies were making huge profits. Financing railways was something new and George Hudson made rules to suit his own

51

purposes as he went along. He became adept at cooking the books. It was great while it lasted, opening a new company to clear old debts with the inrush of new money. However, once saturation point was reached the bubble burst, the railway boom ended and he became bankrupt. He fled to France where he lived like a pauper for 20 years. After his death in London in 1871 he was buried at Scrayingham a village on the Derwent River next below Howsham his birthplace.

Once this revered thrice mayor of York and M.P. for Sunderland (1845-59) had fallen from grace, his name was removed from the Aldermanic record books and Hudson Street was renamed Railway Street. Not until the centenary of his death, 1971, did Hudson Street re-appear in York. It had taken a century for public opinion to mellow sufficiently for people to acknowledge that, for all his financial jiggery-pokery, George Hudson had placed York firmly on the railway map through creating fine railways like the North Eastern. Now, today, the man who started the process of mergers which, in 1923, culminated in four huge companies, L.N.E.R., L.M.S., G.W.R. and Southern is firmly established as the railway king.

Aeons ago, at the end of the Ice Age, water from the melting ice cap formed a lake between it and the eastern side of the Wolds. The overflow from this lake wore away a valley along which more water rushed to spill into Lake Humber on what is now the Vale of York. Today this valley, one of a number of hanging valleys in the area is, for the most part dry, the only stream being a tiny one, a misfit, which starts at Springwells and flows eastwards towards Market Weighton. The valley cuts right through the Wolds from east to west and the Hudson Way follows it.

The stream, part of the long distance footpath, the Wold's Way and the nature reserve all coincide with the Hudson Way as far as Springwells.

The staff and pupils of Market Weighton Secondary School manage the nature reserve on behalf of the Yorkshire Wild Life Trust. Within its delightful confines school parties are encouraged to explore and become involved with interesting projects. Plaster casts of animal footprints are made, bird song is taped, trees and plants are identified, lichen and moss is surveyed and insects living within a given area are classified. All this and more the nature reserve has to offer. The school children are taught to observe the Country Code and to 'take nothing but photographs and leave nothing but footprints'.

The reserve's makers and administrators have good reason to feel proud of their creation for, through it, countless children, and others, will derive great benefit for many, many years to come.

Journeying along the valley the track swings from one side of it to the other, crossing a road by means of a tall brick built bridge. This bridge is unusual in that it has no key stones; and the wonder is that although throughout the life of the line many trains crossed it, they did so in complete safety.

Having crossed this bridge and steadily gained more altitude the track arrives at Kiplingcotes station which from its windy perch, surveys the valley and the gently rolling Wold countryside beyond. The station buildings are solidly constructed and include a rather splendid station master's house, a signal box and a goods shed. Since the closure of the line, the goods shed has had a chequered life first as a venue for discos and currently as a furniture store called 'Grannie's Attic'.

The station is being developed as a picnic area and now tables and benches straddle what was once the siding leading to the goods shed. These tough items of picnic furniture have an interesting story to tell which further illustrates the ingeniousness of Humberside's Technical Services Department. The legs are the boles of fir trees sunk deep into the cinders and the flat surfaces are of elm. When deadly Dutch elm disease attacks, the damage is done to the wood close to the underside of the bark, the timber in the middle of the trunk being unaffected. When a stricken elm is felled, the branches and that part of the trunk wood close to the bark are destroyed but the rest is workable. Using the sound parts of diseased elms, as has happened at Kiplingcotes station, is a success and the result, like the quality of carpets in all the best railway carriages used to be, is first class.

Kiplingcotes station sits on its lonely hillside in splendid isolation, much as it did when trains used to stop there. For throughout its working life most of the passengers entraining there were sheep bound for Beverley Market from the surrounding farms on a one way ticket.

The nearest village is Etton, a small place spread along the roadside some distance away. There is a pond in the middle of the village and a church on a grassy mound dominates its eastern edge. The not too distant village of Middleton-on-the-Wolds has a well kept green on which are seats with no paths leading to them and a notice warning 'Keep off the Grass'. Etton has no such like notices on its grassy bank.

Cherry Burton is much bigger than Etton and some splendid trees grow there including oaks and beeches. There, two hundred years old,

53

Market Weighton to Beverley Line. The bridge with no keystones mentioned in the text

brick built, red tiled cottages and new houses built in traditional style compliment each other rather well. In this pretty dormitory village harmony rules - at least on the surface.

The Wolds slip behind and, rising from a lush verdure of parkland ahead, the graceful, pale towers of Beverley's magnificent Minster entice. This, oldest of the town's buildings is architecturally outstanding in a place noted for the superb quality of its buildings. It all makes a fine climax to a lovely interesting walk and leaves the walker with happy memories of among other things, a modern nature reserve in an Ice Age valley, a keyless bridge, sheep grazing on steep sided Wolds, distant steeples, windy corners, gulls soaring behind a plough and luxurious pastures; oh! and the people we met were really nice, too.

11. THE SELBY TO MARKET WEIGHTON LINE

Length : 17¼ miles
Opened : 1848
Closed : Bubwith station for passenger traffic - 20th September, 1954
Bubwith station for goods traffic - 27th January, 1964
Holme station for passenger traffic - 20th September, 1954
Holme station for goods traffic - 2nd August, 1965.
This was the date of the last regular service along the line but it was used on Saturdays and for holiday traffic until the end of the summer season 1965.
O/S : Sheet 105 and 106 - Scale 1:50,000

> *'No poetry in Railways! foolish thought*
> *of a dull brain, to no fine music wrought.*
> *Charles Mackay*

Selby is the line's western terminus and for the first 6¼ miles across a flat, featureless countryside to where the sluggish River Derwent divides East Yorkshire and Humberside the track is privately owned.

In such pancake surroundings skyscapes in endless variety dominate the scene and, because there is so much sky around, the interested walker of disused railways can quite easily be led, ever so gently into an interesting and rewarding walk-associated hobby: that of weather forecasting. With a little practice, the different kinds of cloud occupying the great vault of heaven can be identified and once classification has been established a stab at determining what weather to expect from them can be made.

Clouds can be divided into three decks, low, medium and high. They are further classified by shape into heap clouds, layer clouds and feathery clouds. Having established these general cloud divisions, a more detailed study will enable you to differentiate between, say, cumulus and stratus, nimbus and cirrus.

Simply by lifting your head as you walk along, a fascinating new hobby presents itself; and there is no better starting place than the low lands of East Yorkshire and Humberside.

East of the Derwent at Bubwith, the track becomes public and remains so until within a few miles of Market Weighton. Embrasured and pinnacled, Bubwith church sits on a wooded bank above a bend in the river at the west end of the village. It overlooks an 18th century, three arched, stone bridge, the village itself, water meadows and a section of the disused railway track. It dominates the surrounding countryside.

The going is easy through this low landscape which seldom rises more than 20 feet above sea level and is always subordinate to the commanding sky. This is because the miles are featureless with few trees to break the skyline.

Holme-upon-Spalding-Moor straddles a road to the south of the track. It is easily identified because its 150 feet high, wooded hill, the only one for miles, stands out against the interminable flatness.

There is a farm on the main road just south of Holme which was built in 1790 as a workhouse for both sexes. Slightly beyond it, a signpost points down a lane which leads in a south easterly direction for two miles to another farm close to the Market Weighton canal. This farm is called 'The Land of Nod'. And to think that throughout my infancy I was led to believe that the land of nod was upstairs.

The track continues from Holme in a north easterly direction to Market Weighton across a broad sweep of plain that reaches from Ouse to Humber and as far eastwards as the low line of the Wolds. It passes through a tame landscape, shaped by the hand of man, so the lines are gentle, because he's made a pretty good job of it. But bitter winds still sweep across it during cold winters. Man may boast that he is in complete control of his environment but, you know, he isn't really, despite those countless rows of root crops. It is nature that is in control, which is as it should be.

12. THE HULL TO HORNSEA LINE

Length   :   15½ miles
Opened :   March 1864
Closed   :   19th October, 1964
O/S   :   Sheet 107 - 1:50,000

> *As we rush, as we rush in the train,*
> *The trees and the houses go wheeling back,*
> *But the starry heavens above the plain*
> *Come flying on our track.*
> *James Thompson (1834-1882)*

Few maps show it, but it is there right enough and the track from Hull
to Hornsea slices right through the middle of it. Holderness is its
name. It is bounded by the River Hull to westwards, Barmston Dyke
to northwards, the Humber and the North Sea; and it is flat. Nowhere
does this low lying land, one of the north's most important corn
growing regions, rise above the 100 foot contour. Its meandering
streams are sluggish and, since the terrain is clay based, its flora is
quite different from that of the adjacent chalk Wolds.

The Hull and Hornsea Railway built the line but the N.E.R. worked
it. For the first three months of its life trains terminated at
Wilmington on the outskirts of Hull, after which Paragon became the
terminus. Much of the traffic was commuters from Hornsea, which
was becoming a dormitory for Hull, although a small amount of
holiday traffic used the line during summer months.

When the line closed Humberside County Council purchased it for
public use and, in time, a cycle track will run the full length of it.
Walkers, joggers and horse riders are being encouraged to use it. To
this end a foot bridge is to be built across Holderness Drain. So, again
it is hats off to the Technical Services Department for enterprise.

The original bridge over the stream at Castle Hill was demolished
when the line closed but until a replacement footbridge is erected a
short detour across a farm bridge will bring you nicely across this slow
flowing obstacle. Guarding the bridge, like Horatius and the two
companions who held back Posena's Etruscan army on the Sublician
bridge over the Tiber, is the farmer's dog. Day after day this fine
creature stands guard. He takes his job seriously, snarling and
barking, and leaping about, giving a most alarming display of
hostility. But there is no need to worry: he cannot hurt you. His chain

is too short.

The first village the track passes is Swine, a dead end, beyond which only tracks lead to low lying farms. Once it was an important pig market.

A priory for Cistercian nuns was founded at Swine in 1150 which, in its own special way, was nonconformist. For when, in 1267-8, Arch Bishop Gifford visited it he was surprised to find monks living on the premises and the lord of the manor paying more attention to the nuns than convention decreed. And if that was not bad enough, the sick were being neglected and the prioress was showing favour-itism. It was much removed from a properly conducted priory where one could imagine the prioress throwing a fit if she found a toilet seat up! This state of affairs, especially of the heart, continued unbridled well into the 15th century. The situation appears to have righted itself by 1539 when the community was dissolved. By then only a prioress and 19 nuns remained and there wasn't a monk in sight.

There are some grass covered mounds in a field to the west of Swine. They and the dominant church are all that remain of those distant halcyon, holy times.

All sorts of goodies thrive along this and other disused railway lines but, since they usually grow in profusion, they are all too often regarded as common and dismissed as distasteful weeds. Yet many of these much maligned plants form the main ingregients of successful herbal remedies.

A doctor may prescribe *Decotium Taraxaci,* which is dandelion root, pure and simple, boiled in water. It is a fine tonic for liver, blood and rheumatic complaints. From the flower of the dandelion a superb wine is made, the leaves add crispness to a salad and, dried, the ground root makes dandelion coffee. Truely the humble pee bed is a wonderful gift from God; and it grows wild along the track.

The finest medicines for high blood pressure contain *Urtica Dioica,* which is another name for the common stinging nettle. In spring the succulent, young leaves of this plant, when boiled with barley, dandelion root and Easter Ledges are absolutely delicious. This herb pudding can be eaten hot or cold, by itself or as a vegetable with a meat course, and if that isn't versatility I don't know what is. Stinging nettles grow in profusion along the track.

The track on its journey north-eastwards to Hornsea crosses a damp terrain where willows grow. Willow bark is used as a cure for rheumatic fever.

Nature make the ailment and nature makes the cure; and so often, these cures are to be found all around the walker who strides along a disused track.

For the ornithologist this walk holds special interest, particularly in winter when great flocks of black headed gulls desert the cliffs and make their noisy way to Hornsea Mere and other stretches of inland water. Large numbers are often seen soaring above this largest freshwater lake in all Humberside and Yorkshire and what a splendid sight it is! But this is only part of the picture, for Hornsea Mere is an important staging post for many types of migrating birds. Canada geese which were originally introduced to this country from North America and today breed wild in many parts of Yorkshire roost at Hornsea Mere together with grebes, herons, swans, teal and many other species. The Mere is leased to the RSPB and there is escorted visiting throughout the year on Mondays, Wednesdays and Saturdays and on Sunday afternoon from May to August inclusive. If you are not an RSPB member you will be charged; but if you do, as I have done, become a member entrance is free. So go on - join. You won't regret it.

Hornsea in the Middle Ages was not nice to know. For in the 13th Century the Abbots of York ruled this small fishing village with a rod of iron. Not content with a cut of the profits from a market they allowed to be held there they levied tolls on ships, wrecks, bread, beer, land tithes and passing strangers. And to ensure that all these dues were collected they built a prison, a pillory and a gallows. So between them the nuns at Swine and the monks at Hornsea excelled in showing the least acceptable faces of monasticism.

Conditions there improved tremendously with the dissolution and continued to do so until, in 1835, Hornsea was acclaimed the most important of Hull's watering places.

In 1949 two brothers started a pottery a mile south of Hornsea which today includes a huge car park, a field for picnicing and a 28 acre leisure centre.

There is no excuse. The walking is easy beneath skyscapes that more often than not are superb and the rewards at the end of it are manifold. So go ahead, best foot forward.

13. THE HULL TO WITHERNSEA LINE

Length   :   20¾ miles
Opened   :   June, 1854
Closed   :   19th October, 1964
O/S   :   Sheet 107 - Scale 1:50,000

> *The smallest train went from view behind the plantation,*
> *Monotonous - but there's grace in monotony.*
> *Edmund Blunden*

The Hull to Withernsea line was constructed by the Hull and Holderness Railway and opened in June, 1854. For the first ten years of its life its Hull terminus was the former York and North Midland station at Victoria Dock. Then, on 1st June 1864, almost exactly 10 years to the day since the line was built, trains began running from Paragon Station. As with the Hull-Hornsea line, this one's main traffic was residential with some holiday traffic to the seaside in the summer months.

For little more than half its length eastwards from Hull, the track is owned by Humberside County Council, which means that this 'with it' authority has gained a hat-trick - Hudson's way, the Hornsea line and this.

Three miles of flat walking separate Hull from Hedon, whose station, now gone, was built to the north of and just inside the old borough boundary, with its goods shed lying just outside it. This was done deliberately for old medieval rights allowed the borough to take tolls on all goods unloaded within its bounds. Because the Hull and Withernsea Railway Company had no desire to pay tolls on goods they unloaded at Hedon they built the goods shed where it can still be seen today, just outside the old borough boundary.

The Hull to Withernsea branch, possibly more than any other disused railway line in England, is qualified to use the appellation 'Royal' and for this reason. Near its Hull end, the magnificent 130 feet high tower of St. Augustine's church is known as the 'King of Holderness', and roughly three quarters of the way along it, Patrington's lovely, slender spire is known as the 'Queen of Holderness'.

Hedon is one of England's oldest boroughs. It received its first charter in 1170, but long before it was granted its fourth charter in 1272 its importance as a commercial port on the Humber had passed to Hull. Its church, which really is superb, was built at the end of the

12th century when Hedon's prosperity was at its greatest. Its style is Early English Gothic and, thanks to its famous tower which gives it a touch of dignity, it looks like a small cathedral. In a part of England renowned for its beautiful churches, St. Augustine's stands proud - pinnacles and pierced parapet above the rest.

If antiquity does not cling to the name 'Hedon' the town's barred layout smacks of the 12th century, as do the street names - Churchgate, Fletchergate, Souttergate - and the triangle of open ground in Market Hill where the old twice weekly markets were held.

Walking across a flat landscape, having journeyed in places as diverse as the Pennines, the Lake District, the North York Moors, the Wolds and the Vales of Pickering and York, makes me realise just how lucky we are in Britain to enjoy a countryside of such enormous variety. For variety is what makes walking along a disused railway track - or a road, or a faint mountain trod or a contour or a compass bearing - so infinitely rewarding. Every journey is at least three journeys, one physical, one historical and one spiritual; and the latter is perhaps the most important; especially if the walk is close to the walker's home. Because all too often it is in the landscape of his home ground that he, or she, discovers his deepest spiritual experiences. The walker is remade within the country side, its familiar characteristics holding an undefined comfort for him. As to the mountain man, mountains are held in awe, so are the flat, fenny lowlands of Holderness to anyone living there. All this stems from the fact that *homo sapiens*, no matter what else he believes in, emphatically believes in himself and his place in Nature. No matter how he pollutes it, for the most part, man believes that the countryside is his true home.

The track runs to the south of Burstwick, a village with some interesting historical associations. A castle one mile north west of it was once the seat of government for Holderness. Both Edward I and Edward II are said to have lived there and the wife of Robert Bruce was once imprisoned in it. Now all that remains of this once proud pile is its moat.

'My uncle', a local told me, 'was a passenger in a train travelling in the vicinity of Burstwick when the ill-fated airship, R38, burst into flames over the Humber and crashed. It was the one and only time he would rather not have had a grandstand view.'

South east of Burstwick the track, now private, curves very gently to Patrington, passing a mile to the north of Ottringham, another village with a fine steeple.

Patrington's glorious, 189ft. high spire beckons from miles away, soaring as it does towards heaven from a flat landscape. It beckons this 'Queen of Holderness', in a most delightful way and the heart leaps at the beauty of it. Building began on the church at about the end of the 13th century and was completed about forty years later.

Patrington village is a harmony of carved stone. Everything about it blends, nothing clashes. It is a lovely spot.

The flattest landscape in Holderness lies to the south of Patrington. It is a sombre landscape of low horizon and large fields flanked by drains. Fine cereal crops are grown in these fields which, until 1831, when they were reclaimed, were Humber siltlands. The few scattered farms to be found in this parish of Sunk Island, no part of which is more than 15ft. above sea level, are all more then 100 years old. They are built of red Holderness brick and have slate roofs.

Pink-footed geese which feed on the Wolds can often be seen around Sunk Island, although their usual roost is at the National Wildfowl Refuge on Read's Island, further up river and close to the Lincolnshire shore.

However, back to the track, which now takes a north-easterly direction to Withernsea, parallel to a drain. No roads are crossed; there are no level crossings between Patrington and Withernsea. What there is, in abundance, is sky. It dominates and dictates the quality of the walk by its mood.

There used to be a pier at Withernsea but during a severe storm in October, 1830, a coal barge sailed through it, causing some 200ft. of the structure to break away. This was repaired but in March 1882, another severe gale removed that part of the pier the previous gale had not damaged. Now only its stone pier towers remain. Withernsea is an ordinary seaside resort with promenade, an entertainment area, a sand and shingle shore and the sea is usually cold. It is the walk along the disused line that gets you there that is rather extraordinary.

II. West and North West Yorkshire

The Vale of Mowbray, running the full length of Yorkshire from north to south, divides the Pennine uplands on the west from the Wolds, the North York Moors and Holderness to the east. It is a broad, fertile and gently undulating, agricultural region wherein lie picturesque villages and old fashioned towns like Northallerton and Thirsk. Northallerton is reputed to be one of the richest towns in England. It is situated close to where the Battle of the Standard was fought.

West and North West Yorkshire is a complex which can be divided roughly into the lowlands of the east and the Pennines of the west. To the south west of the region, where the land rises to become the Pennine Moors, farmland merges into a broad, manufacturing belt which penetrates the valleys and cuts into the rolling heights. It is a region of many industries, thousands of firms and tens of thousands of people. It is, as Defoe said 'a noble scene of industry and application', and wool textiles dominate. Yet in those valleys, where encroaching industry has become established, much of the original beauty remains and the extensive moors are as untouched and brooding as they have ever been.

As these industries developed, great numbers of people were attracted to them. They were to be found for the most part, south of the Aire, grouped around deep valleys on the Pennine foothills. Workers were recruited from all corners of the British Isles and abroad. Most West Riding towns had their Irish colonies.

At first the woollen industry, the iron and steel manufacturers and others used canals for the conveyance of raw materials and finished products. Then, when it was seen that the canals could no longer cope with the growing volume of traffic, the railways were built.

Today many of those once busy branch lines are silent and still. The polished tracks along which fussy engines used to haul their loads have now been raised and Nature is busily reclaiming her own.

North of the Aire, the Yorkshire Dales were, and still are, almost entirely rural; and their open spaces attracted tourists. In 1846 the first railway to encroach on the Dales was the Darlington to Richmond line. Thus the North Eastern brought people to within walking distance of Swaledale's beauties. In 1849 the North Western carried tourists from Skipton and Lancaster to Ingleton and the route was quickly extended to Kirkby Lonsdale and Sedbergh. A branch from Northallerton, built by the North Eastern reached Leyburn in 1856 and Hawes in 1877. One from Leeds and Bradford to Ilkley was opened in 1865. This was extended to Skipton from where the Yorkshire Dales Railway ran to Grassington. Other lines followed including the little Nidd Valley Light Railway, which was built originally to serve the builders of the Upper Nidderdale reservoirs. The line reached the hamlet of Lofthouse in 1907.

By far the most spectacular of all the lines through the Dales was the Settle to Carlisle, built by the Midland Railway Company. Its construction was railway engineering at the very best. At one point the track is carried across bleak Ribblehead on a long and renowned viaduct, the largest man made structure in the Dales. The line is still in daily use but under threat of closure because of soaring maintenance costs.

Those same lines which helped to establish tourism as a major industry in the Dales also helped to delay the decline of other local industries. But the delay was short lived. Now many rail links between the Dales and the sprawling industrial centres of South West Yorkshire have passed into history. But all is not lost. The disused railways now offer a chance to all who have the ability and the will to walk, with permission where necessary, in the steps of those railway-men who played so important a part in the development of West and North West Yorkshire.

Two of the 'Devil's Arrows' at Boroughbridge

14. THE CROSS GATES TO WETHERBY LINE

Length : 10½ miles
Opened : 1st May, 1876
Closed : For passenger traffic - 6th January, 1964
For goods traffic - 4th April, 1966
O/S : Sheet 104 - Scale 1:50,000

> *A rush of steaming hedges,*
> *Of jostling lights and shadows,*
> *Of hustling, hurrying stations,*
> *Of racing woods and meadows.*
> *W.E.Henley*

When the line was opened it was to the old station at Wetherby, which was closed on 2nd July 1902, when the direct curve from south to west was opened, giving a direct run from Leeds to Harrogate. Wetherby's new station was used from then on to replace the defunct original one.

Cross Gates was a junction on the Leeds to York line and the line to Wetherby leading from it went straight into a cutting. Today this cutting is filled in and the first station along the disused line as it climbs to the summit, is Scholes, now a public house and restaurant.

To the north of Scholes, once the summit is crossed, the long gradual descent to Wetherby via Thorner, Bardsey and Collingham Bridge begins.

Many of the houses in this area are built of tough, abrasive gritstone.

Every village has at least one cricket pitch; and inhabitants without a profound insight into the game are rare as web-footed hens. For in this part of the world, as throughout Yorkshire, cricket is a religion. The local is as proud of his cricketing knowledge as he is of his local brew, his Yorkshire fare and the scenery. Show a genuine interest in cricketers like Len Hutton, Fred Trueman and Geoff Boycott and you will quickly reach his heart and find the measure of his hospitality.

Sometimes the way is all muddle and confusion, cutting, as it does at times, through a tangle of things lost within other things, brambles tumbling across fallen branches, spiky tendrils worming into crevices and dandelions pushing through the exposed ribs of a dead rabbit. All this is part and parcel of the living world and everywhere within it a strange beauty is to be found. This beauty of the living world is universal and stops only when it reaches Man.

Bramham Park lies to the east of the old line, midway between Thorner and Bardsey. It is a Queen Anne mansion, built on classical lines and set in 70 acres of gardens. Built by the 1st Lord Bingley between 1698 and 1711, it is still occupied by his descendents. The grounds are landscaped in the style of Versailles and the mansion contains some exquisite porcelain, fine pictures and furniture. Every spring and summer it is open to the public and is well worth a detour, if only to remind ourselves that in the days before cricket, in its present form, was invented, Yorkshire had something even more civilized and longer lasting to offer than the crack of the ball on willow.

The Wetherby-Crossgates line crossed the River Wharfe at Linton. The railway bridge is gone and walkers must take a short detour over this stone road bridge.

15. THE HARROGATE TO PATELEY BRIDGE LINE

Length :   14 miles
Opened :   1st May, 1862
Closed :   For passenger traffic - 2nd April 1951
              For goods traffic - 31st October 1964
O/S :   Sheets 99 and 104 - Scale 1:50,000

> *By falling stream and standing hill,*
> *By chiming tower and whispering tree.*
> *A.E.Houseman*

The Harrogate to Pateley Bridge line was an important country link, which became even more important when the Nidd Valley Light Railway was built in 1907. For an end on connection from the N.E.R. Pateley Bridge station enabled mineral and goods traffic destined for the extensive Bradford City water supply projects higher up the valley to be looped onto it.

Today its stations are no more and the track itself has a five o'clock shadow; but these are small blemishes when set against the great joy of following the course of this once busy line through a green and pleasant valley.

Not many disused lines can boast as posh a departure point as Harrogate, England's first 'watering place' and now a thriving, floral conference centre. Harrogate has come a long way since that day in 1576 when William Slingsby discovered the first chalybeate spring in the then hamlet of Haywragate, 'the road passing near the park'. It has survived because it has changed its life style. No longer a spa where people take the waters, it has become an important centre for Dales visitors, a place where important events like the annual Great Yorkshire Show are held. How easy it is to linger there; but the old track calls.

At first the way is northerly, curving north-east towards Dragon Junction, beyond which it swings back to north. Then, at Bilton Road Junction, it turns towards the north-west, first along an embankment then on the level to where a viaduct once carried the railway over the River Nidd. Alas, the viaduct has been demolished. Still, it is well worth walking to the truncated southern portion of the viaduct because the views from there up and down stream are rather fine.

Having admired the view it is a matter of retracing your steps to the southern end of the embankment, where a road goes under the track. Turn right along this road for a mile to the A59, where turn right again and go to a junction with the A61. Again turn right along this road to Ripon for two miles to rejoin the disused railway track once the River Nidd has been bridged.

You are now a mile and a half away from the northern end of the now vanished viaduct and bang on course. The way is to westwards.

After four miles the first intermediate station, Ripley Valley, is reached. Originally is was named Killinghall and shown as being three miles from Harrogate in the original timetable; but it wasn't long before the name was changed to Ripley. Then it was announced that the station would be called Ripley Castle. However, before this could be effected there came another change of mind by those in authority and from 1st April, 1875 the station took the name Ripley Valley, which it kept throughout its life. It is now a private residence.

A mile and a half further upstream and still on the river's north bank is Hampsthwaite, the only intermediate station without goods facilities. It, too, is now a private residence.

Of the remainder, a small housing estate has been built on and around the site of Birstwith station, Darley is being redeveloped and Dacre is a private residence.

Midway between Birstwith and Darley the route crosses to the south bank of the river and returns to the north bank midway between Dacre and Pateley Bridge.

At Dacre a two miles diversion across the river, through Summer Bridge, straight across the B6165 and along a lane will bring you to Brimham Rocks, one of the most amazing of Yorkshire's natural phenomena.

Brimham Rocks is a heather covered site comprising over 60 acres where huge gritstone rocks, some weighing 500 tons, tower in shapes so fantastic that earlier generations thought that they had been sculpted by Druids. But the Druids had no hand in it. A violent upheaval in carboniferous times pushed the rocks to the surface on this site on the edge of the Vale of Nidd, where, once exposed to the elements, wind and sandstorms did the shaping. At that time there were neither trees nor heather on the site. These came later and today picnickers sit among them and marvel at shapes like the Dancing Bear, the Baboon, the Druid's Writing Desk and other weird figures. Of them all perhaps the most mind-boggling is the 200 tons of Idol Rock, which is delicately balanced on a column only twelve inches in diameter. I doubt if there is another place quite like Brimham Rocks in England. So see it if you are able. You will not be disappointed.

Because it winds its pleasant way through a pastoral landscape where dry stone walls and farm buildings blend gently into the countryside, and since a lovely river keeps it company throughout most of its length, this walk has a lot to offer. On a fine summer's day when the air is warm but not hot enough to shimmer distance and sunlight sparkles on flowing waters the experience of striding along the track can be very pleasurable indeed.

Pateley Bridge, which means 'badger's field', was once a small village, now transformed by lead and iron mining into a small town. It is an excellent walking centre and the start of the famous Nidd Valley Light Railway, which, for the explorer of disused railway lines, makes an excellent sequel to the Harrogate to Pateley Bridge line, itself a fine walk in its own right.

View down Nidderdale from Glasshouses. The course of the railway can be seen across the centre.

69

16. THE NIDD VALLEY LIGHT RAILWAY

Length : 14 miles
Opened : For goods traffic - 11th September 1907
For passenger traffic - 12th September 1907
Closed : Autumn 1936
O/S : Sheet 99 - Scale 1:50,000

> *Now I reach the mountain's brow*
> *What a landscape far below;*
> *No clouds no vapour intervene,*
> *But the gay, the open scene,*
> *Does the face of nature show,*
> *In all the hues of heaven's bow.*
>
> *John Dyer*

What a pity the Nidd Valley Light Railway never survived the 1930's because, had it done so, the likelihood is that droves of railway buffs would be patronising it today. Such enthusiasm is well earned for, without doubt, this spanking little line, which nosed its scenic way into the very shadow of Great Whernside, was much loved. Many visitors to Pateley Bridge thought it was the finest light railway in all Yorkshire, and put their tickets where their tongues were to prove it.

At the turn of the century a company called Power and Traction Ltd. applied for authority to build a 2ft. 6inch gauge light railway from Pateley Bridge to the village of Lofthouse, seven miles up the valley. The application was granted but the necessary capital was not forthcoming so the construction could not begin.

At that time Bradford Corporation was involved with the second phase of their city water supply project. Phase one, the building of Gouthwaite reservoir, was complete, and phase two, the building of Angram reservoir and dam, was in progress. The main Angram site was seven miles further up the vale than Lofthouse and, at first, was served by a private road built on Bradford Corporation land.

As work progressed it was found that this road could not cope with the volume of traffic required of it. Other means of supplying Angram site had to be found. Bradford Corporation solved the problem by taking over the authority to build a light railway from Power and Tractor Ltd. The corporation's only use for the line was to carry materials to the Angram site but, in order to comply with the Light Railway Act, it also had to provide a passenger and goods service between Pateley Bridge and Lofthouse.

The gauge was changed from narrow to standard but the rail remained of light proportions, 56lb. per yard of flat bottomed profile. The first sod was cut in July, 1904, and on the 11th September 1907 the line was opened. It was unique because it had become a passenger line worked by a municipality.

Phase three, the building of a huge reservoir at Scar House, began in October 1921. It was so vast a project that a village had to be built to accommodate the 700 man strong labour force. Thirteen locomotives, twenty five locomotive cranes and four steam navvies were also used on this massive undertaking. The railway's job was to supply the site with all its requirements except stone for the dam which was quarried north of the valley and 500 feet above it.

Once the Angram job was finished, the railhead was cut back three miles to Scar House. Regular workmans' and supply trains continued to run there until 1936 when that reservoir was complete. Scar House reservoir was opened officially on 7th September of that year and it marked the beginning of the end for the Nidd Valley line. Soon after the opening of the former the latter closed.

In 1937 the track was lifted.

Today little remains of this rather special little line, which is a pity. If only it hadn't closed when it did what an attraction it could have become. If only....but the world of what might have been is built on if onlys.

The busy, little line did close. Long past is its heyday which saw five passenger and three workmens trains travel the line each way with goods trains carrying cement, coal and other site requirements, slotted between them. No longer do the classic 4-4-0 tank engines - named Holdsworth and Milner after Bradford worthies - and others of their like chuff along 1 in 40 gradients and through a tunnel cut into limestone to reach Angram.

There is not much left now. Change has left its mark. Wath and Ramsgill stations are private houses. The large wooden building that housed shops while Scar House reservoir was being built has gone. Once the cattle which grazed in the dry stone wall enclosed fields around Ramsgill were all shorthorns. Today they are fresians.

Yet the lonely Nidderdale moors remain, as do the kestrels, the buzzards, the merlins, the lapwings and the skylarks, who were there before the railway came. Sheep still roam the 'heafs' they settled on a thousand years ago. In fact it is thanks to the sheep that the fells have not become forests. With their constant grazing they have prevented the tree seeds from regenerating naturally, thus ensuring that the moors, like Nidderdale, keep their characteristics of space, wide open views and immense skies.

The Nidd Valley Light Railway ran through some fine Dales country. Yet it never belonged to that famous part of Yorkshire. For when the Yorkshire Dales National Park was founded, Nidderdale was not included in it. Is there no justice?

View of Pateley Bridge from across the valley.

17. THE PILMOOR TO KNARESBOROUGH LINE

Length : 13 miles
Opened : Pilmoor to Boroughbridge - 17th June 1847
Boroughbridge to Knaresborough - 1875
Closed : For passenger traffic - September 1950
For goods traffic - 1964
O/S : Sheets 104 and 106 - Scale 1:50,000

Here is a child who clambers and scrambles,
All by himself and gathering brambles.
Robert Louis Stevenson

The child has grown old and is dead and gone like the rails: the brambles remain like the space between them; and from the remains of an old branch line a new walk has evolved.

Prior to 1847 Boroughbridge, an important coaching town on the Great North Road, had no rail connections. Then, in that year a branch line was opened with the sole object of serving the Boroughbridge area. It came complete with a new station, Pilmoor, at its eastern end, which provided connections between trains working the branch and slow trains on the main line.

In those days Yorkshire was divided into Ridings. Boroughbridge was in the West Riding, but sitting on the boundary. When the station came to be built it was in the North Riding!

There was one intermediate station on the line, Brafferton, which, because it served an extensive, rich, agricultural area, became more important than Boroughbridge. Time, however, that great leveller, has redressed the balance. Today both stations are deserted and derelict.

In 1875 the branch was extended to join the York-Harrogate line at Knaresborough and the time tables were duly arranged so that connections were met.

The extension caused severe civil engineering problems because a continuation to the original line could not give sufficient clearance over the nearby roads to Dishforth and Catterick Bridge. To overcome this difficulty a new line was built which branched from the original one to the east of Boroughbridge station. This allowed the new line to gain sufficient height to cross the above two roads without making the rail gradients too steep to be worked. The old station was converted into cottages, although the goods shed remained in use throughout the

73

line's lifetime, and a new Boroughbridge station was built on the fresh section of the track.

No part of the old railway is ever very far from a road so anyone wishing to sample a particular section of it can do so with ease. For anyone walking its full length there are only two places where slight detours are unavoidable. One is at Brafferton where the rail bridge over the Swale has been removed. The other is at Boroughbridge where the rail bridge over the Ure has gone. At both places the detours are easy to follow.

From Brafferton station take the road south into the village where, at a junction, turn right and walk westwards until you reach the Swale. Cross it over a footbridge and take the path immediately on your right which will return you to the track.

From Boroughbridge station go through the town, crossing the Ure, and take the Roecliffe road to where it crosses the old track - and voila!

These diversion directions are for people walking in a westerly direction.

Not to be outdone by the rich landscape through which it cleaves, the track provides a glorious display of wild flowers which change with the seasons. They come in an infinite variety of colours and shapes, these delightful plants, covering stark bareness with a living coverlet that softens and brings harmony to the scene. As one season's flowers fade others take their place, making a vivid cavalcade of things natural that is as long as the year itself.

One of the first plants to flower in the spring along the trackbed is the coltsfoot with its bright yellow flower heads. Another is the lesser celandine. From April to November the herb robert displays its clear, pink flowers. May sees the red campion in bloom, attracting bumble bees and hover flies. Flowering at the same time is the ragwort with its golden yellow flowers. Disused railways seem to be as attractive to ragwort as it is to the black and yellow caterpillars of the cinnabar moth. Horses and cattle take a more jaundiced view of this striking plant because if eaten by them it can cause an obstruction of the bile - jaundice, which can be fatal. Daisies, so called because their flower heads open in the daytime and close in the evening, abound. So does the great plantain, which grows where nothing else will grow. Come autumn the toadflax is flowering and fruit hangs heavily on the bramble and dog rose.

Many more species of wild flowers can be seen growing along the Pilmoor-Knaresborough track. They attract all sorts of wild creatures which, in turn, attract others. This is the way Nature works, this is all part and parcel of its complex make up and this is what puts interest into walking disused railways.

An extra couple of hours spent at Ripon will allow the railway
walker to sample the equally fascinating delights
of canal walking, along the full 2¼ miles
of the Ripon Canal

18. THE HARROGATE TO NORTHALLERTON LINE

Length : 28½ miles
Opened : 1848
Closed : 6th March, 1967
O/S : Sheets 99 and 104 - scale 1:50,000

> *Oh, the wild engine!*
> *The cutting, the embankment; how it takes*
> *The tunnels, and the clatter that it makes;*
> *So careful of the train and of the track,*
> *Guiding us out, or helping us go back.*
> Harold Munroe

There are no tunnels along this stretch of disused track but there are plenty of cuttings and embankments, and no two are exactly alike. Details vary from mile to mile and the only real way to see them is on foot. When passenger trains rushed along this once busy line it was usually the wide vistas that caught the traveller's eye, not the wealth of detail which flashed past so quickly it became blurred. Now that the track has been lifted those special details so often missed from a carriage window can be studied at leisure by anyone walking along the track bed.

For the first 4½ miles from Harrogate station the same track serves the Pateley Bridge and Northallerton routes. Thus the detour detailed in the chapter on the Harrogate to Pateley Bridge line applies equally to this route. Where the Pateley Bridge track is reached, on the north bank of the River Nidd, turn right and go in an easterly direction for ¾ mile to where the Pateley Bridge and Northallerton lines merge. Now turn left and begin walking in a northerly direction, spot on course.

The hills of Wensleydale, which lie some 30 miles to the north west of Harrogate, resemble giant staircases. This topography, which is responsible for the many fine waterfalls in the area is formed by alternate layers of soft mudstones and much harder sandstone and limestone many hundreds of feet thick. It is called the Yoredale Series and its fringes touch Harrogate where, on the eastern side of the cutting near the station, remains of Lower Carboniferous limestone can be seen.

The deep, wooded gorge a good three miles north of Harrogate station, through which the Nidd flows, is not the river's embryonic course. Its original valley was a wide one and the contrast between it

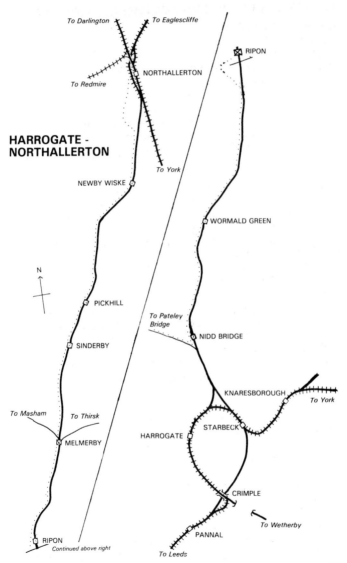

HARROGATE - NORTHALLERTON

To Darlington

To Eaglescliffe

RIPON

NORTHALLERTON

To Redmire

To York

NEWBY WISKE

WORMALD GREEN

N

PICKHILL

To Pateley Bridge

SINDERBY

NIDD BRIDGE

KNARESBOROUGH

To York

To Masham   To Thirsk

HARROGATE   STARBECK

MELMERBY

CRIMPLE

To Wetherby

RIPON   PANNAL

Continued above right

To Leeds

and the gorge, which was the result of glacial pressures, led to the elucidation of the glacial lake phenomena in Yorkshire then, later, throughout all England.

Nidd Hall, which is a mile north of the demolished viaduct over the Nidd gorge, stands on the moraine of the Vale of York glacier, the west end of which, at an early stage, lay high up into the flanks of the Pennines. To the north of Nidd Hall the track cuts through this moraine.

At Wormald Green the track, which is still on the moraine, cuts through some magnesian limestone and a lot of loose superficial deposits called drifts. This is the last cutting before four miles distant Ripon is reached.

Ripon, Yorkshire's smallest city, is dominated by its cathedral, a rather severe edifice, built of millstone grit. To anyone approaching Ripon along the track from Harrogate the cathedral's towers, seen from a distance, are a sight to behold, especially in hot weather. For cathedrals and churches attract pubs like hedgehogs attract fleas, Seldom will you find one without the other.

The same cannot be said for what used to be Ripon's railway station, which has been converted into a caravan park. However, don't let that put you off. Ripon has a lot to offer and an exploratory dalliance could prove very rewarding.

Although the outside of Ripon's minster church may be dour the inside is anything but: and the wood carvings are marvellous.

It was Saint Wilfrid, appointed Bishop of York in 669, who founded the cathedral and the old place has survived the ravages of centuries rather well.

Cromwell's troops stabled their horses in the cathedral nave en route to London with Charles I where he, the King, was executed. The King himself spent the night in the stables of a house since occupied by an aunt of Naomi Jacob, the Ripon born novelist.

Smack in the middle of Ripon is the market square, which Daniel Defoe called the most beautiful in England. At nine o'clock every evening a ceremony is performed in the square which had its beginnings in the days of Alfred the Great. A man wearing a tricorn hat and carrying a great curved horn sounds the horn once in each corner and once in front of the Mayor's house. This is called 'setting the watch', a custom which originated when Ripon had a Wakeman who, for a fee of two pence per door per year insured the citizens against their houses being robbed between the setting of the watch and sunrise.

There is no wakeman today but the 13th century wakeman's house, now a museum, still looks out on the square and his office is remembered in the citys motto: 'Except the Lord Keep the city the Wakeman waketh in vain'.

When leaving Ripon, take the road bridge over the Ure and immediately turn left, then right at a fork in the road to rejoin the disused track to Northallerton.

There is some subsidence on each side of the track both to the north and south of Ripon. This is due to the melting, over many centuries, of the soft gypsum the ancient rocks originally contained.

For four flat miles the way is almost due north up the Yorkshire plain to Melmerby in the Vale of Mowbray where the V.O.M. pies come from.

Melmerby was originally a wayside station but when the link to Northallerton was opened in 1852 it became a junction station. Then, in 1856, following the construction at Northallerton of a curve which joined the Great North of England (east coast main line) and the Leeds Northern Lines, through trains to Teesside were directed via Thirsk, up the Great North of England to Northallerton and then along the curve back onto the Leeds Northern line. Not until 1901, when the line was doubled, did the Melmerby to Northallerton link become an important route.

From Melmerby our way is north directly to Northallerton, leaving the routes east to Thirsk and west to Tanfield and Masham to be the subjects of other walks.

There are still 13 miles to go but the terrain is flat, the going is easy and well within the compass of an experienced walker. However, there is nothing to stop anyone so wishing to split the walk into three sections, each roughly 9½ miles long.

Throughout, we are on a featureless drift-plain, but over to eastwards the Hambleton escarpment catches the eye as do the high moors of the Pennines to the west. Soon after the half-way point is passed we cross the River Swale - yes, the bridge over it is still there - close to the village of Maunby and, ere long, reach five miles distant Northallerton, capital town of North Yorkshire and its administrative centre. It may be a flat town, this once important railway junction, sitting pretty on its flat plain, but it is far from being flat broke. For, of its size, it is one of the richest towns in England.

19. THE MELMERBY TO THIRSK LINE

Length   :   5¼ miles
Opened   :   1848
Closed   :   September, 1959
O/S   :   Sheet 99 - Scale 1:50,000

> *As we rush, as we rush in the Train,*
> *The trees and the houses go wheeling back,*
> *But the starry heavens above the plain,*
> *Come flying on our track.*
> *James Thompson*

The Melmerby to Thirsk line is not a branch: it is the top end of the main line from Leeds to Thirsk and is an interesting walk. Beginning at Melmerby and moving in an easterly direction across the pancake flat Yorkshire plain, two miles distant Leeming Lane is soon reached. This is part of the great Roman road, Dere Street, which slices across the featureless plain in a N.W.-S.E. direction, straight as the flight of an arrow. This most interesting old road is worthy of more than a passing glance and a climb onto the bridge which carries it over the disused railway track is recommended. Roman Leeming Lane was 'all composed of stone and paved with large 'coggles', river boulders, which the neighbouring inhabitants take away to build withal and pave their yards, etc'. In the early eighteenth century turnpikes were set up and as coach travel developed the road became the principal coach road to the North of England. Today the road has been modernised but its romantic associations remain.

A lot of wheat is grown east of Leeming Lane for hereabouts arable farming is assisted by high July temperatures and a not too heavy average annual rainfall.

A mile beyond the unnatural Roman road, the natural river Swale snakes along on its southerly course. The contrast between road and river illustrates an old truth: that whereas man is obsessed with straight lines, in Nature the opposite is the case.

The Swale is crossed just south of Skipton-on-Swale and some three miles further on a curve to the north leads directly to Thirsk station.

The Leeds and Thirsk line had its own terminus in the centre of Thirsk, but it was short lived. It closed as such, circa 1855, being used from then until it closed in October, 1966, as a goods station.

Thirsk's G.N.E. station, is out in the country, 1½ miles west of the town on the east coast mainline. It lies at the top end of the afore-mentioned curve from the Leeds and Thirsk line and the end of this nice, little walk.

Known today simply as Thirsk, it used to be known as either Thirsk Junction or Newcastle Junction. In fact it used to be a very different station from the one seen there today. For it has been rebuilt since the days when the authorities of the G.N.E., the York, Newcastle and Berwick Railway were at deadly enmity with those of the Leeds and Thirsk Railway and the Clarence Railway group. Although the curve linked both lots of lines, the G.N.E. people were most uncooperative. At first the G.N.E. Authorities would not have a covered platform at Thirsk; nor would they receive any cattle wagons from the Leeds and Thirsk line. Worse, they did all they could to discourage transfer of goods by this route by charging high rates. It makes you wonder why they allowed the curve to be built in the first place. It takes all sorts doesn't it?

20. THE MELMERBY TO MASHAM LINE

Length : 7½ miles
Opened : 9th June, 1875
Closed : for passenger traffic - 1st January, 1931
for goods traffic - 11th November, 1963
O/S : Sheet 99 - scale 1:50,000

> *I like to see it lap the miles,*
> *And lick the valleys up.*
> *Emily Dickinson.*

The branch was a short lived one and it had only one intermediate station, Tanfield, which at the outbreak of World War II served six villages, 57 farms and a flour and cake mill; and its main traffic was agricultural. But the war changed all that. The area became a storage point for ammunition and from 1941 to the cessation of hostilities traffic increased tremendously; but it was predominantly military. So much so that the Army provided troops to assist the small railway staff. The soldiers lived in a camp set up opposite the station. Because of its wartime military importance permission was granted for limited lighting so that urgent traffic could be handled in the black out. In the six weeks prior to D-Day 42 special trains used the branch. At the end of the war it took 17 trains to remove the 750,000 land mines remaining in the West Tanfield area.

Slightly over four miles of easy walking from Melmerby will bring you to Tanfield with its interesting past. Sadly, the station is derelict but the village, sitting prettily on the bank of the Ure, is well worth a visit.

Just as Tanfield became deeply involved with the Army, so Masham became deeply involved with the Harrogate and Leeds Corporations. In 1901 Harrogate Corporation began work on a reservoir at Roundhill some five miles south west of Masham. The materials for this project were brought to Masham by train from where they were trans-shipped by lorry to a depot at Leighton. From there a two foot gauge railway carried the materials to the site. This arrangement proved unsatisfactory because the road surface suffered severe damage and in 1904 the narrow gauge railway was extended north eastwards from the Leighton depot to terminate just across the road from the N.E.R. Station. In 1905, the North Eastern Railway authorities provided a siding from Masham station to the Harrogate Corporation depot across the road. This was to ease the trans-shipment of goods from standard gauge N.E.R. wagons to the narrow gauge ones owned by Harrogate Corporation.

When Roundhill reservoir was completed circa 1910 the narrow gauge railway was taken over by Leeds Corporation which was building adjacent Leighton reservoir. The outbreak of the 1914-1918 war brought work on the reservoir to a halt. The huts were commandered and at first were used to house the West Yorkshire Regiment. As the war progressed German prisoners of war were billeted in them. After the war work was resumed on the reservoir and it was completed in 1925. At that time the plant was sold but the narrow gauge line was not dismantled until 1930 or thereabouts. Since this line was lightly constructed, little of it remains today.

Following the closure of the passenger service in 1931, the Masham branch was served by a daily No.1 braked goods from Leeds but this ceased after two or three years. There was also a daily pick-up goods.

In 1962 the M.P. for Darlington complained in the House of Commons that the Masham branch was being kept open solely to supply fresh water to some of the gate houses and coal for the Masham station master to sell as he was entitled to do under a long standing agreement going back to N.E.R. days when station masters were allowed to run a coal merchants business.

The line closed on 11th November 1963.

Throughout its length the Masham branch is on limestone grassland. This proffers richer feeding than the corresponding natural pastures of the acid soils but it doesn't have the value of good lowland pastures. Sheep love it since the dryness of this limestone grassland minimises two of their principal ills, liver fluke and foot rot. The area is well suited for sheep grazing.

These limestone based trackside pastures offer a wealth of flowers as varied as Autumn gentians, cowslips, milkwort and primroses, all of which delight the eye.

Ah, yes! And there are plenty of hedges, which is as it should be, for as Richard Jeffries said in 1884: 'without hedges England would not be England'.

21. THE WENSLEYDALE LINE: REDMIRE TO GARSDALE

Length : 18 miles
Opened : For goods to Askrigg - 1st February 1877
For goods to Hawes - 1st June 1878
For passenger traffic to Hawes - 1st October 1878
For all traffic Hawes to Garsdale - 1st October 1878
Closed : Hawes to Garsdale - 16th March 1959
Redmire to Hawes:
For passenger traffic - 24th April 1954
For goods traffic - 27th April 1964
O/S : Sheet 98 - Scale 1:50,000

> *See beacon'd penhill, view to stately rise,*
> *Whose scalling altitude invades the skies;*
> *Go climb its brow, its airy tracks explore.*
> *Thomas Maude*

This beautiful Wensleydale branch was extended by the North Eastern Railway Company, under an Act of Parliament of 4th July, 1870, from Leyburn to connect with the Midland branch running from Hawes Junction to Hawes. This historic event took place on 1st October 1878, when the link between the east coast route at Northallerton and the Settle-Carlisle route at Hawes Junction became a reality.

Hawes Junction was Garsdale's original name. In January 1900, the Midland Co. changed it from 'Hawes Junction' to 'Hawes Junction and Garsdale' and in April 1933, to 'Garsdale (for Hawes)'. As if this wasn't sufficient, the station was renamed 'Garsdale for Hawes and Northallerton line' in the 1950's. The Midland Co. similarly tried to change the name of Hawes Junction loco shed but the L.N.E.R. authorities would have none of it and the shed retained its original name until it was closed on 1st May 1939.

Thanks to the successive alternations of shales, flagrock, limestones and grits which its slopes present from the bed of the River Ure, at 500ft. to the fell ridges, over 2,000ft. high, Wensleydale has a varied and very rich plant life. Below Aysgarth it has about it a breadth and freedom which no other dale can equal. Throughout its length the dale's natural advantages are evident: the scenery is beautiful and the views are magnificent.

Lead mining was declining by the time the line west of Leyburn was opened; but the agricultural wealth of the dale was developing. Milk

The River Ure, Marmion Tower and church at West Tanfield

also played an important part in the every day working of the branch, as did Wensleydale cheese and butter. The great importance the railway authorities attached to the butter traffic is illustrated by an instruction in 1900, to the Midland goods due to leave Hawes at 3.25pm. to 'waite at Hawes till butter ready Tuesdays'. The line, in fact, got much more revenue from passengers and cattle than it did from goods and minerals.

There was one special occasion, in 1927 when a natural phenomenon caused the greatest influx of traffic the line had ever seen. In the early hours of 29th June a total eclipse of the sun took place. The centre line of the belt of totality ran across the north east of England. Leyburn was a popular viewing point and excursions from as far away as Kings Cross, Norwich, Colchester and many other places converged on the place from both east and west.

Redmire, where the walk begins, is a quiet village, pleasantly situated in the heart of Wensleydale between tree shaded Bolton Hall Park and, a mile to the north west, Castle Bolton, home of the Scropes, one of the most powerful families in medieval England. It was to Castle Bolton that Mary Queen of Scots was brought in 1568, in the custody of Lord Scrope, Warden of the Western Marches, to whom she had surrendered at Carlisle.

The route goes through a cutting as it passes below this massive pile and a detour to make a closer inspection of the Scrope seat is strongly advised.

Fresh from its confining cutting, the track, now on an embankment, swings southwards in a great loop towards Aysgarth. The surrounding fields are lush and the hedges and trees a delight to behold. A mile to the west of the track as it pulls out of the loop lies the village of Carperby, birthplace of the famous Wensleydale sheep. The village was once a centre of Quakerism and was visited by George Fox.

A stop at Aysgarth is a must. The name is Norse and means 'a clearing among oaks'. But neither the clearing nor the oaks is the main attraction. That distinction goes to Aysgarth's truely magnificent falls, of which there are three distinct sets. The Upper or Horse Shoe Falls have a mill race lying across the top of them. It used to supply water to Yore Mill, just below the fall and which is now a museum. The museum faces a modified pack horse bridge which makes a good viewing platform for the Upper Falls. The Middle Falls, reached by a footpath along the north bank of the river, are a few hundred yards downstream of the bridge. Still further down are the Lower or North Falls where the Ure spills over a series of limestone terraces. When in spate the sight is awe inspiring.

Leaving Aysgarth the vale becomes steeper, narrower and more confining. The disused line continues up it, hugging the north bank of the Ure; and yard by yard the excitement mounts, stimulating the adrenalin.

The next station on the line is Askrigg, once famed for its knitters. Askrigg also went in for clock making, brewing, cotton spinning and dyeing. It used to have a market but that died when Hawes assumed prominence when a turnpike was constructed at Askrigg. Old now, the village carries its age well. As Ascric, meaning 'Ash-ridge' it is mentioned in the Domesday Book.

Between Askrigg and Hawes the track, still skirting the river's north bank, passes through a landscape of such breathtaking loveliness that there is a strong desire to tarry a while and drool. Yet almost unbelievably the surroundings continue to improve the closer you get to Hawes. Downstream of this busy market town the track crosses to the south bank of the Ure where it remains all the way to Garsdale. The bridge has been demolished but a little further upstream there is a convenient road bridge. Cross it and in next to no time you will be passing Hawes station, now a National Park Information Centre.

On most summer days the station yard is packed with the cars of tourists inspecting the station precincts and its displays. Platform One is a botanist's paradise and there are fish for the catching in a stream at the end of Platform Two.

With the infant Ure and the A684 for company the track heads for six miles distant Garsdale. Only now the landscape has changed dramatically. Gone are the lush meadows and pastures, so plentiful around and below Hawes. Instead the track is hemmed in by steep, windswept moorland slopes, wild, brooding and oh so beautiful when seen beneath scudding clouds.

This vivid change in scenery is really not so surprising when you consider that Garsdale is one of the remotest stations in the dales. So explosed is it to fierce winds that the tale is told of an engine being spun round on the turntable by the wind force alone. In winter, snow storms have always been part of living at Garsdale. They are an expected hazard and many a time have engines been stuck in funnel high drifts.

Therefore, do the walk in summer and if you feel in need of refreshment at the end of it, the Moorcock Inn is not far away.

This walk really is a top notcher. It positively screams to be tackled again and again. Its bountiful offering of glorious scenery, great variety of flora and fauna and its romantic appeal and historical associations make this walk one that takes some whacking.

22. THE RICHMOND LINE:
FROM ERYHOLME JUNCTION

Length : 10 miles

Opened : 10th September 1901

Closed : For passengers - 3rd March 1969

For goods - Catterick Bridge to Richmond - 3rd March 1969

For goods - Eryholme to Catterick Bridge - 9th February 1970

O/S : Sheet 98 - Scale 1:50,000

There MUST be dales in Paradise
which you and I will find
And smile (since God is kind)
at all the foreign peoples there
Enchanted by our blessed air!

A.J.Brown

Although Richmond station was a railhead for the lead mining industry in Swaledale, both Richmond town and the line itself have always had strong military associations. Those of Richmond town go back 1,000 years and long before Catterick Camp was opened, during World War I, annual military camps were held in the Richmond area. On those occasions a great many special trains were run to convey the large numbers of troops attending the camps.

At the other end of the line, at Eryholme Junction, the station was closed in 1911 but the branch platforms remained in use for those railway employees and their families who lived in that isolated spot. Then during World War II the station was used by R.A.F. personnel from a nearby airfield.

From Eryholme Junction the track crosses a flat, agricultural landscape in the general direction of S.W. At Catterick Bridge it changes direction to west and at Broken Brea level crossing it follows a S.W. course. When just two miles short of Richmond it makes a swing to N.W. in order to remain in the valley of the Swale.

For the first eight miles or so the track is privately owned and permission must be sought before using it. At one point it has vanished under a caravan park. Only the section from Easby to Richmond is designated a public footpath. Fortunately, this is the most picturesque part of the whole route.

There were three intermediate stations along the line, of which

The oldest surviving stone castle in Britain is at Richmond.
Visitors can climb to the top of the tower
up some dark and narrow stairways

Catterick Bridge was by far the most important. The other two, Moulton, 2½ miles from Eryholme, and Scorton both became unstaffed halts. Today Scorton station, which is situated a mile away from Scorton village, is a pub.

When Catterick Camp was built during World Ward I it was linked to Catterick Bridge station by a four miles long spur. Leaving the goods yard west of Catterick Bridge station in an easterly direction the line swung round to S.W. before crossing the River Swale on a girder bridge. It then went due west to a terminus in the camp two miles south of Richmond station. This line was know as the Military Camp Railway.

During both World Wars many thousand of troops passed through Catterick Camp and most of them were carried to and from the camp by train. Even in peace time the passenger traffic was heavy. Every weekend leave specials were run to cities in all parts of the country.

July 10th 1957, was a happy and memorable day for the line because the Queen travelled along it when visiting Catterick Camp. She arrived at Catterick Bridge in a train pulled by an engine aptly named 'Bon Accord' but completed her journey with two Ll 2-6-4 T engines pulling the royal train along the Military Camp Railway.

However, not all the events along the line were happy ones; and two in particular were very sad. On 15th September 1917, a set of coaches filled with troops moved off down a gradient and coaches were derailed at various places along the line. Four men lost their lives including one who survived the derailment only to be knocked down by another train.

At 4 p.m. on 4th February 1944, while troops were loading ammunition at Catterick Bridge for the D. Day offensive there was an explosion and twelve people including the station master, were killed.

Richmond station with its overall roof and its scatter of outbuildings was a cut above the general run of small railway buildings. Although now an agricultural showroom the best thing about it is its situation at the foot of Swaledale proper. Had it been built at the dale's head and been called Keld the scar the line would have made along the delightful River Swale would have seriously affected the narrow dale's natural beauty. Nor would the line, had it been extended, have contributed greatly to the vale's needs. Although disused railways can be put to many excellent uses, Swaledale can count itself lucky not to have one.

90

Richmond from the bridge outside the station

III Durham
(With just a pinch of Tyne and Wear)

For many centuries until 1974, when the county boundaries were redrawn, hilly County Durham was surrounded by Northumberland to the north, Cumberland to the west, Yorkshire to the south and the North Sea to the east. As a direct consequence of these boundary changes County Durham lost two large industrial complexes and gained, at Yorkshire's expense, a long finger of land which included the whole of beautiful Upper Teesdale.

Of the two industrial regions lost, one is a coal mining and ship building area which spreads along the coast from below Sunderland to well above the old Northumberland border. It has become Tyne and Wear. The other has become County Cleveland. It is the home of I.C.I.'s giant petro-chemical division and of British Steel's huge Redcar works. It embraces the whole of the Tees estuary and reaches inland almost as far as Darlington. It includes what was the flattest land in County Durham. Contrary to popular belief among many people who have never been there, County Cleveland does not have a single coal mine.

From the wild Pennines along County Durham's western boundary three rivers flow eastwards to the North Sea. They are the Tyne, which forms part of the Northumbrian border, the Wear, which meanders across the middle of the county and the Tees which, until 1974, marked the boundary with Yorkshire's North Riding. The upper courses of these rivers are famous for their wooded dales, which make a striking contrast to the surrounding high moors.

Although the climate can be harsh in winter, a high proportion of the land is cultivated; oats, wheat and barley being the principal crops. There is dairy farming in the dales and sheep farming on the moors.

County Durham is also heavily industrialised, its economy being based on the coal field which occupies a third of its area and stretches from the eastern edge of the Pennines to the coast and under the sea.

With the growth of the railways in the 19th century, industrial development became rapid. Transport facilities along the three main rivers grew as the railway network expanded. Today County Durham's main industries are concentrated near the eastern section of the coal field.

The economic depression of the 1930's led both before and after the Second World War to the establishment of new industrial areas like Newton Aycliffe and Peterlee.

Before the Romans came to County Durham it was, historically, a desert; a no-man's land with little evidence of settlement. Then from the 7th Century the church began to take an important place in the county under Cuthbert, patron saint of Durham and the Venerable Bede. By the later Middle Ages the bishops had become so powerful they were the only authority capable of maintaining order in that turbulent area. Durham therefore gradually emerged as a County Palatine with the bishops wielding considerable administrative and judicial power. Not until Henry VIII came to the throne were these powers curtailed.

There are several mediaeval castles in the county, notably Barnard Castle and Durham itself. At Durham Cathedral there is the finest example of Early English ecclesiastical architecture in the country.

It was in County Durham that, on 27th September 1825 the world's first passenger train, Locomotion, made its historic journey from Shildon to Darlington and Stockton. Thus was born a mode of transport which was to revolutionise the civilised world. Within a decade of the opening of the S. & D.R. the advantages of carrying goods and passengers by rail had been proved.

Although the building of the S. & D.R. was due to the efforts of many people - engineers, craftsmen and thousands of navvies - three men, Edward Pease, Jonathan Backhouse and Francis Mewburn deserve special mention for had it not been for their tenacity and conviction the S. & D.R. might not have been built and Darlington would have never made a name for itself as a railway town and come to be remembered as the birthplace of all railways.

Edward Pease was a Darlington Quaker who became known as the father of the railways. It was he who managed to persuade another Quaker, the influential Darlington banker, Jonathan Backhouse, that the proposed building of the S. & D.R. was a sound one. Once persuaded, Backhouse raised much of the capital. Another Darlingtonian, solicitor Francis Mewburn drew up the vital Acts of Parliament authorising the construction of the line. Once the S. & D.R. was operational, he acted, as a solicitor to the Company and in so doing became known as the world's first railway solicitor.

Since it was in at the beginning, County Durham is proud of its railway heritage. In village pubs locals tell rare tales of once proud lines that are no more; and their eyes light up as half forgotten memories are recalled.

Contrasting sharply with the disused lines of County Durham's eastern industrial areas, which are grotty, are the splendid rural ones, especially those of the western uplands. They meander around a landscape for all the world like a crumpled patchwork quilt, wander up sylvan vales and climb windy Pennine heights. They offer mile after mile of exhilerating walking. People in need of a euphoric experience should try them. They will not be disappointed.

23. THE BARNARD CASTLE TO KIRKBY STEPHEN LINE

Length : 23 miles
Opened : 4th July, 1861
Closed : 22nd January, 1962
O/S : Sheet 92 - Scale 1:50,000 M726

I will lift up mine eyes unto the hills;
From whence cometh my help.
Psalm 121

This trans-Pennine line, which rejoiced in the name 'the South Durham and Lancashire Union Railway', was a subsidiary of the Stockton and Darlington Co. It was built to transport iron ore from Lancashire to the blast furnaces on Teeside and to carry coal and coke on the return journey. At first the line, which had its western terminus at Tebay, was a single track; but this was doubled in three stages, in 1867, 1873 and 1874. The widening of the track necessitated the re-building of three of the viaducts along the route.

Barnard Castle station is now a tennis court. Between it and the River Tees to westward the reception area of Glaxo laboratories sits squarely across where the line used to run. The fine viaduct, 732ft. long and 132ft. hight, which once carried the line across the Tees, has been demolished and high walls have been built across the track at each truncated end of it to prevent foolhardy humans and stray cattle from falling over the edge and being killed.

It is best, therefore, to start the walk from the western stump of the viaduct, which is easily reached from the town centre by using the road bridge which spans the Tees just below the castle. Once across, turn right and continue upstream for half a mile. The remains of the viaduct are clearly seen from some distance. Once there you will see a track leading up the embankment to the trackbed. Climb it and turn left, go along the disused track which for most of the way to Lartington, a mile and a half distant, is a continuation of the embankment you have just climbed, and you are on course for a great adventure.

The surface is ash and the walking is easy through a harmony of green fields wick with wild life. There is an abundance of wild birds and the air is clean.

In common with many disused lines a lot of the farm underpass bridges have been removed. But it is not beyond the wit of a

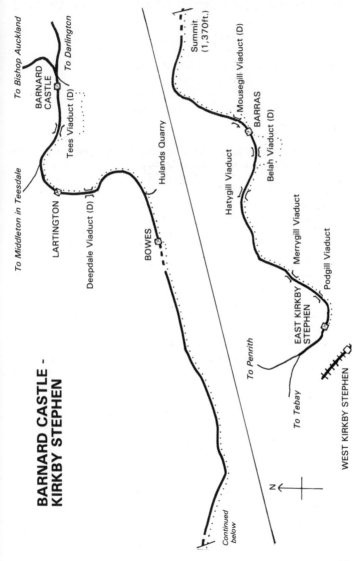

**BARNARD CASTLE -
KIRKBY STEPHEN**

To Bishop Auckland

To Darlington

BARNARD CASTLE

Tees Viaduct (D)

To Middleton in Teesdale

LARTINGTON

Deepdale Viaduct (D)

Hulands Quarry

BOWES

Summit (1,370ft.)

Mousegill Viaduct (D)

BARRAS

Belah Viaduct (D)

Hatygill Viaduct

Merrygill Viaduct

Podgill Viaduct

EAST KIRKBY STEPHEN

To Penrith

To Tebay

WEST KIRKBY STEPHEN

N ←

Continued below

The Market Cross at Barnard Castle

determined person to square up to and overcome such small obstacles. They are an integral part of walking disused railways and must be expected.

West of Lartington the track swings south and merges with the rough road to Cat Castle Quarries. But where the quarry road takes a S.W. direction the track continues due south, to cross the narrow well wooded vale of Deepdale. When the line was operational a metal structured viaduct crossed this beautiful valley; but, alas, it has now been demolished.

Deepdale without its viaduct is a bit difficult to cross; but once this has been accomplished, the way once again becomes straight forward. It continues in a southerly direction, first through a mile long cutting, then under the A67 before curving W.S.W. to follow a course roughly parallel and just out of sight of the A67.

Just west of Bowes station the track is swept under the dual carriageway of Bowes village by-pass. What a pity the station had not suffered a similar fate. It looks ghastly standing there all forlorn, slowly decomposing, its glassless windows staring like sightless eyes across a platform half hidden beneath a thick stubble of weeds. The station has lost most of its slates which, one suspects, is precisely what happened to those in authority who chose to leave it standing while opting to demolish three of the line's lovely and useful viaducts.

The track can once more be identified as such a little way to the west of Bowes and the best way to get there is through the village itself.

Bowes is old. It stands on the site of a Roman station called Lavatrae, which was built to guard the desolate pass over Stainmore. The Normans built a castle there of which all that remains is its large four square keep. Towards the top end of the village, near the cemetery where lies the body of the original Smike, is the building that became Dotheboys Hall in Dicken's Nicholas Nickleby.

For seven glorious miles the track climbs gently towards Stainmore summit and for most of the way it has the infant River Greta for company. For the first few miles it clings to the side of the shallow valley and, because of this, the northern aspect is restricted by rising ground. To the south the views are much more expansive and a sheer delight to behold. The contrast between the well husbanded farms of the valley bottom and the surrounding fells is marked.

Some two miles west of Bowes there are two bridges: one, under which the track goes, is man made while just below it, there is a natural limestone bridge, God's Bridge, beneath which the Greta flows. The Pennine Way crosses both of them.

Gradually, as the head of the valley is approached, the farm buildings fall behind and the fields, now mainly rough-pasture, shrink and are gone, swallowed by ubiquitous peat moors.

For all the world like a huge dollop of black dough that has risen and split in the process, boggy Stainmore is home to a wealth of wild life. Here foxes abound, as do stoats and weasels and the hares and rabbits on which they prey. This, too, is the land of the curlew, the snipe, the partridge, the kestrel and the red grouse.

Spread across the bedrock of millstone grit at a high altitude and kept wet by mists and moderately heavy rains, the peat moors offer ideal conditions for heather, bilberry, crowberry, cotton grass, sheep's fescue and other acid loving plants.

Aeons of wear have split some of the smooth surface of the moor into detached peat hummocks known as peat hags which, given a few more centuries of weathering will, like ourselves, have gone.

At Stainmore summit both signal box and track have gone, smothered by a new road improvement scheme. This means crossing the summit on tarmac; but in less than a mile the track is rejoined as it begins its spectacular descent of the Pennine's western escarpment.

What follows is really top drawer stuff for as the track curves towards Barras it offers panoramic views of the Upper Eden Valley that are as good as if not superior to anything any other disused railway can offer; and that's saying something.

All that remains of the once proud bridge which spanned the road to Tan Hill, England's highest pub, slightly north of Barras, is a yawning gap. Stand close to the edge of it, overlooking tall trees and the vast spread of the Eden Valley and the chances are your head will spin. Stand too close and you could be on your way to Heaven. It is much better, and safer, to gaze on this sight from the safety of the road which will bring you to Barras station and back on course.

Barras was the highest station in England and from it the views of the Eden Valley and the confining Pennines were, and still are, magnificent.

A little to the south of the station is the very picturesque, steep sided Belah Ghyll across which Mr. Bouch flung an iron viaduct, 1,000ft. long, 196ft. high and with a 60ft. span. It had 16 iron pillars and a stone buttress at each end. To cross it in a swaying light engine during a snow storm, as happened to the author, is a frightening experience, exacerbated by the knowledge that the same Mr. Bouch built the Tay Bridge which collapsed.

Now only the buttresses and the pillar supports remain. All else has gone including a document which had been placed inside the centre column of the eighth pier when the viaduct was built. This document gave details of the viaduct's construction and ended with this piece of verse:-

> *To future ages these lines will tell*
> *Who built this structure o'er the dell -*
> *Wilson with these eighty men*
> *Raised Belah's Viaduct o'er the glen.*

One wonders if this document has survived Belah's downfall, and if it has, where it is today.

There are two cuttings between Barras station and Belah Ghyll. Between them a farm road goes S.E. along a contour to one mile distant High Ewebank farm from where a path leads downhill to cross Belah beck before it drops into the Ghyll. The path climbs the opposite bank and arrives at Wrenside farm from where another farm road, going roughly eastward, rejoins the disused railway half a mile south of Belah Ghyll at Belah Cottages. This detour adds about 1½ miles to the walk but it is a very interesting one and nothing like as ardous as a direct crossing of Belah Ghyll.

West of Belah Cottages part of the track is fenced to form a narrow rectangular 'field'. If permission to cross is sought it will almost certainly be given for the local farmers are kind and reasonable folk.

At one point just past where a farm road from Rookby Scarth farm cuts under the track beneath a now demolished bridge and goes off at right angles, downhill, towards Winton, young trees have grown right across the track bed, forming a thickish barrier. This slows progress somewhat but the track soon begins to look more like its old self again.

As the track winds its airy and scenic way down the escarpments it crosses two ghylls, Merrygill and Podgill, which are separated by a cutting. In springtime this cutting is ablaze with massed clumps of primroses, cowslips, celandines and all mannor of beautiful wild flowers.

The woods beneath Podgill viaduct are blue carpeted with wild hyacinths and their fragrance is sweet and good.

There are three stone viaducts between Belah and Kirkby Stephen, Hatygill, Merrygill and Podgill, all of which were originally built only wide enough for a single track. In the 1890's these were doubled by building identical viaducts alongside them, the two being so closely keyed as to give the appearance of a single structure.

This railway walk par excellence is surpassed only by the warmth of the welcome you will receive at journey's end. Kirkby Stephenites are renowned for the warmth of their hospitality. This walk is very highly recommended.

24. THE BARNARD CASTLE TO MIDDLETON-IN-TEESDALE LINE

Length : 8¾ miles
Opened : 11th May, 1868
Closed : 28th November, 1964
O/S : Sheet 92 - Scale 1:50,000

The small train rounded the bend
Watched by us pilgrims of summer, and mostly by me -
Edmund Blunden

Although station to station the distance is 8¾ miles, the first part of the walk, which coincides with the South Durham and Lancashire Union Railway, is brought to an abrupt end because the viaduct over the Tees is no longer there. So, as with the S.D.L.U.R. walk to Kirkby Stephen, the best starting point is from the western stump of the Tees viaduct. Thus the actual walking distance is reduced to eight miles.

For the first half mile the S.D.L.U.R. track is the way. Then, at Tees Valley Junction, where the S.D.L.U.R. curves to the S.W. and Lartington, the Tees Valley Railway shoots off at a tangent N.W. to Cotherstone, Romaldkirk, Mickleton and Middleton-in-Teesdale. From Tees Valley Junction the old track meanders through a most attractive country side, always keeping to the western side of the river and twice crossing stone viaducts over feeder streams.

When the promoters of the Tees Valley Railway applied for and got Royal assent to build the line from Tees Valley Junction to Middleton they hoped eventually to extend it to join the Alston branch at Haltwhistle. But because the line served a thinly populated area it was not a financial success and within a few years the directors were making overtures to the N.E.R. to take it over. In 1880, by which time the N.E.R. had increased its stock holding from £25,000 to £31,000 an agreement was reached under which terms the N.E.R. undertook to settle outstanding debts incurred by the Tees Valley Railway Co. up to the value of £22,000 and to purchase the line for £25,188.

The line benefited greatly from carrying stone from Ord and Maddison's quarries at Middleton. The Lunedale Whinstone Company's quarry close to Middleton station and the Cargo Fleet Iron Co. Ltd's. quarry at Mickleton. More traffic was brought to the branch by the construction of the Baldersdale and Grassholme reservoirs.

By 1873 the number of passenger trains had doubled to six in each direction daily. By the outbreak of the first World War this had increased to seven each way daily with one extra train on Wednesdays and two extra on Saturdays. Circa 1949, when the railways were nationalized there were still six trains each way, only now they worked far beyond the line to places like Darlington, Durham, Sunderland and Newcastle.

At the end of the line Middleton, with its sandstone houses and whitewashed cottages, makes an ideal centre for exploring Teesdale. High Force is a delightful six miles away, upstream, and, further up still is spectacular Cauldron Snout.

At one time Middleton was a frequent prize winner in the annual Best Kept Garden competition; but today its bloom has faded, which is a pity. Mickleton station, on the other hand, has been developed by the County Planning Dept., Durham as a picnic area.

At each end of the line there is access to existing public rights of way. So not only is the walk itself a grand and exhilerating one, its destination lives up to the walks promise, which is a pretty good arrangement.

25. THE DARLINGTON TO BARNARD CASTLE LINE

Length : 15 miles (from Hopetown Junction)
Opened : 8th July, 1856
Closed : 5th April, 1965
O/S : Sheets 92 & 93 - Scale 1:50,000

> *Blessings on Science, and her handmaid Steam!*
> *They make Utopia only half a dream.*
> *Charles Mackay.*

The birth of the Darlington to Barnard Castle line was difficult. It followed a prolonged gestation which began as early as 1767 when it was proposed to build a canal from Stockton-on-Tees to Winston, a village six miles east of Barnard Castle. A feasibility report was prepared in 1768 followed by others in 1815 and 1818, by which time it was realised that, since coal would be the main traffic, the western terminus should serve the west Durham coal field rather than the agricultural area west of Darlington. From this reasoning the Stockton-Darlington Railway was conceived and built to George Stephenson's plans and Winston and Barnard Castle were left in the cold.

Once the S & D Railway had become established, the people of Barnard Castle urged for a branch to serve their town and in November, 1832, a deputation saw the S & D Railway directors. The visit came to nothing because the Duke of Cleveland, who owned a lot of land to the east of Barnard Castle was not sympathetic to railways.

In 1842, following the Duke's death, his son, who succeeded him, saw to it that there was no change of attitude because, like his father, he was anti-railway.

Ten years later, in 1852, another deputation from Barnard Castle sought the help of the S & D Railway directors. This followed a survey which showed that a line could be built between Darlington and Barnard Castle which would cross only a few of the Duke's fields. The Duke, on being shown the scheme, first looked favourably at it; but then he changed his mind and opposed it. Meanwhile a provisional committee had been formed and it decided to submit a Bill for the line; but it was rejected. Then a strange thing happened. Another survey was carried out by a Mr. Bouch, who dressed his assistants as sappers and miners to avoid recognition. However, they were spotted and Mr. Bouch had to apologise personally to the Duke. This he did and at the interview the Duke surprised him by saying that he would

Piercebridge near Darlington is an old Roman Settlement.
These remains are of the bridge which once crossed the
Tees, but the river has since altered course
50 yards to the north

withdraw his objection to the building of the line if it did not pass through Selaby Park. This meant that the proposed line would have to cross both the Tees and the main road twice between Gainford and Winston instead of by a single crossing of the Tees at Langley Beck.

Now competition came from a completely different source - the proposers of a line between Bishop Auckland and Barnard Castle; but this was rejected in Parliament.

The Darlington and Barnard Castle Railway Act was passed on 7th April, 1854. Royal assent was given on 3rd July, 1854 and sixteen days later the first sod was cut. The Darlington to Barnard Castle was on its way.

The track, as it wends its way through the very pleasant countryside to the west of Darlington, has nothing much to offer in the way of engineering or physical features. It is the physical features of the countryside itself that provide the attractions of this lovely walk.

To reach Hopetown Junction, the start of the walk, go along Whessoe Road to Elm Tree Street, on the left, immediately after passing the Rolling Mills. Continue under the railway bridge ahead and along the road to where it bends to the right. There, on the left, a public footpath signposts the way along a lane to Hopetown Junction. Follow the railway line on your left for about 200 yards and continue past the line's buffers until the site of a demolished bridge is reached. Turn right at the road for 50 yards, then cross the road and go along a

The fine stone bridge over the Tees
just west of Gainford

lane leading to a bridge carrying the disused track. Go up the embankment onto the track and then right along it, past Darlington Chemical Works and out into open country.

Four and a half miles from Hopetown Junction the first intermediate station, Piercebridge, is reached: only today it is a private house lying a little to the north of Piercebridge village on Roman Dere Street.

Piercebridge, which means 'withy bridge' is built on the foundations of an important fort erected to guard the bridge carrying Dere Street over the River Tees. The original fort was constructed circa AD125, during Hadrian's reign and later, after AD297, when the northern defences were strengthened, a new fort was built to the west of Dere Street. What a pity Roman scandals are outside the compass of this book.

A couple of pleasant miles further west, in the pre-Norman Conquest village of Gainford, stands a private dwelling, all that remains of Gainford station.

Much of the village edges a very pretty green and like a church hymnal, is a delightful mixture of ancient and modern. The church is particularly interesting and succeeds one built in the 9th century by Ecgred, Bishop of Lindisfarne. Gainford Hall is a much more modern structure: it is Jacobean.

Winston Station, once so neat and trim, is now an untidy transport depot situated about a mile north of Winston village, set deep in rustic splendour. It sits alongside the B6274, a country road leading from Winston to Staindrop, a long pleasant village that, it is said, was given, along with Staindropshire to the Bishop of Durham by King Canute.

Raby Castle, which adjoins the north side of Staindrop is the largest medieval castle in County Durham and one of the most impressive in England. The Nevilles had their seat there until, in 1569, following the collapse of the Rising in the North, their estates were forfeited to the Crown. It was then acquired by the highly political Vane family who purchased it together with Barnard Castle for a total of £18,000. A detour to see it and its herds of deer is well worth the effort.

In keeping with the rest of the track, the four miles from Winston to Broomielaw are pleasant ones.

Broomielaw station served the now empty camps situated to the north of the line and to which, during and for some time after World War II, hoards of soldiers, many drunk or without tickets or both, would return after a night in Darlington.

The drill was simple. Those involved would leap from the carriages as the train slowed on approaching the platform and dive for cover in the shrubs before scurrying hot foot to their respective camps. The Military Police, fully aware of what was going on, often lay in ambush ready to pounce on those unsuspecting troops as they leaped from the carriages. Yes, many a bloody battle was fought at Broomielaw: Many a head was cracked in these frequent confrontations between the revelling soldiers and M.Ps.

Two further miles will bring you to Barnard Castle, the end of a splendid walk. And what better way to cap it than a visit to magnificent Bowes Museum. It is enormous, 300 feet long and 120 feet wide, with larger terraces and pavilions and it looks for all the world like a huge French town hall. In it is housed one of the finest art collections in England.

Ah! The places to which these railway walks lead!

26. THE FORCETT RAILWAY

Length : 5 miles
Opened : June, 1867
Closed : for public traffic - 2nd November, 1964
for quarry traffic - 7th February, 1966
O/S : Sheet 92 - Scale 1:50,000

> *That railways are inadequate appears*
> *Indupitable now:*
> *John Davidson*

This southern pointing spur, which branched from the Darlington-Barnard Castle line at Forcett Junction, to the east of Gainford, and crossed the River Tees on a fine, stone viaduct, was built to provide a goods service to the agricultural area south of the Tees and transport limestone from Forcett quarries to the blast furnaces at Middlesbrough.

Forcett quarries are to be found on the outskirts of the village of East Layton. They are still worked, only these days they are served by road transport.

For many years the line was privately run, greatly helped by the N.E.R. who had one of their clerks seconded to the Forcett company's goods depot. Eventually, in 1923, the L.N.E.R. took over completely. The line was closed in 1966 and has changed little since then.

From the now demolished viaduct over the Tees the track runs southwards for a couple of miles towards Eppleby, where the quarry locos were serviced in an engine shed which is still standing. Then it curves westwards to skirt the western side of Forcett Park and continues to its rural terminus.

Surrounded as it is by lush farmland, the track makes an interesting and exhilerating walk through a part of the country once ruled by the Brigantes, who had a vast encampment near Eppleby.

A road going N.N.E. from the middle of East Layton divides after half a mile. To the west of this bifurcation is the southern terminus of the line and it is a far better starting point than the northern junction because of the missing viaduct over the Tees.

However, if the river is low, it is possible to cross the ford at Gainford and continue up the lane ahead to take the first turning on the left which leads to Low Field farm, from where the line can be easily reached, provided permission is asked for and given to cross Low Field land.

27. THE BARNARD CASTLE TO SPRING GARDENS JUNCTION (WEST AUCKLAND) LINE

Length : 11 miles
Opened : 1st August, 1962
Closed : 12th June, 1962
O/S : Sheet 92 - Scale 1:50,000

> *And here is a mill, and here is a river;*
> *Each a glimpse and gone forever!*
> Robert Louis Stevenson.

This attractive walk from Barney - the locals never call it Barnard Castle - provides an interesting optional extra once Lands viaduct is reached. Most of the route has been acquired by Durham County Council, who intend to reclaim it as a public footpath before selling the land back to the adjoining owners. Their decision to reclaim this old line as a public footpath rather than a walkway was made because of lack of car parking facilities along the line and the fact that it does not pass close to any main roads.

At first the way is along the Barnard Castle-Darlington line, but very soon, at Barnard Castle East, it branches to northwards and curves gently to the north-east to 7¼ miles distant Cockfield Fell Station. Within three miles the first of two stone built viaducts, Forthburn, is reached and a good mile further on is the second, Langleydale. Langleydale viaduct, 411 feet long and 76 feet high, is almost twice the length and nearly double the height of Forthburn; and both are still standing.

Tiny though it is, Cockfield can boast at least one famous son. Jeremiah Dixon, the brilliant, self-taught mathematician was born there. He was the first man to use coal gas for artificial light and shared the job of deciding the famous Mason-Dixon boundary line between the lands of Lord Baltimore and William Penn. In this way Dixieland jazz owed its name to a man from County Durham.

From Cockfield Fell station the line continues north easterly along the north side of Cockfield Fell, descending steadily until, after a mile, the stark remains of Lands viaduct are reached.

Thereabouts the aspect is very open and the views are good, particularly from the top of the Lands viaduct buttress with the river Gaunless winding through its confining tree dotted valley far below.

The viaduct, which slants across the river in a spectacular way, had four iron spans, each 120 feet long, supported by three piers built of

*The beautifully situated Langleydale Viaduct between
Barnard Castle and West Auckland*

brick and stone. The piers remain but the girders have been removed. It is 640 feet long and, at its maximum, 93 feet high.

From Lands viaduct there is a choice of routes and the previously mentioned interesting optional extra. The more direct and less exciting way is down the steep valley side, across the river, which is shallow enough to be forded except in flood, up the other side and back onto the track. Now it is simply a matter of continuing along it for a further three miles, passing Evenwood after 1½ miles to Spring Garden Junction and the end of the walk.

The alternative is much better. Edging the river Gaunless is the track of a much older line called the Haggerleases branch. It was opened on 1st October, 1830, to carry coal traffic from the maze of coal workings along the valley bottom. Originally horses pulled the coal trucks and when, on 27th November, 1848, the Stockton-Darlington engineer was asked what it would cost to replace horses with a small locomotive, the reply was that it would be prohibitive. Not until September 1856, were locomotives used on the branch.

On September 1st, 1899, the name of the terminus was changed from Haggerleases to Butterknowle. It remained open as a coal depot until September, 1963.

Today the river Gaunless flows through a silent valley, past piles of rubble, all that remains of a once busy coal mining area. Today the wind combs a valley empty of all except a few sheep and a lot of memories. Yet it needs little imagination to see the valley when it was a hive of industry. So the detour upstream from the viaduct is very rewarding because those crude remains stimulate the thirst for knowledge.

When you return to Lands viaduct continue along the track under it, downstream. After about three miles, at the top of an incline, you will reach Spring Garden Junction and the end of an interesting walk.

Site of Westgate station. Route of line is clearly shown:
Wearhead extension.

28. THE WEARHEAD EXTENSION
(THE WESTERN SECTION - WESTGATE TO WEARHEAD)

Length :   3½ miles
Opened :   Stanhope to Wearhead - 21st October, 1895
Closed :   Westgate to St. John's Chapel:-
              For passenger traffic - 29th June 1953
              For goods traffic - 1st November 1965
              St. John's Chapel to Wearhead:-
              For passenger traffic - 29th June 1953
              For goods traffic - 2nd January 1961
O/S   :   Sheet 92 - Scale 1:50,000

> *I hear a local train along the valley. And 'There*
> *goes the one-fifty', I think to myself.*
> *Siegfried Sassoon*

The Stanhope to Wearhead extension of the Weardale branch was the third and final stage of a line running east to west up this remote Pennine valley. The first stage, from Wear Valley Junction to Frosterley, was opened in 1847, the second stage, from Frosterley to Stanhope, was opened in 1862 and this was extended to Wearhead in 1895. As far back as 1844 it was envisaged that the line would run beyond the head of the valley and on, through a 2½ miles long tunnel, to Alston and Brampton to link with the Newcastle and Carlisle Railway but nothing came of it.

It was the mineral wealth of Weardale that attracted the railway promoters. Bronze, iron, lead, limestone, silver and zinc were all mined there and to the railway promoters this meant good business hauling it, especially the iron ore and the limestone. Today much of the intense industrial activity has gone and, certainly from the west of Stanhope, pastoral peace and serenity has once more settled on this mediaeval hunting preserve of successive bishops of Durham.

Lovely Stanhope, situated midway along the dale, would have made a convenient starting point but for the line which continues for some distance to serve some quarries. The walk, then, begins at Westgate which is higher up the dale than the quarries, beyond which the track has been lifted.

Weardale is glacial and, in places, only a few hundred yards wide. Dry stone walls wander up and across its steep sides and here and there lofty, craggy escarpments soar.

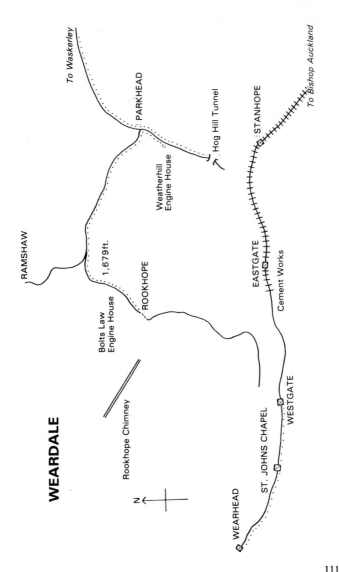

WEARDALE

To Waskerley

PARKHEAD

Hog Hill Tunnel

STANHOPE

To Bishop Auckland

Weatherhill
Engine House

RAMSHAW

1,679ft.

ROOKHOPE

Bolts Law
Engine House

EASTGATE

Cement Works

WESTGATE

Rookhope Chimney

ST. JOHNS CHAPEL

N ←

WEARHEAD

Upper Weardale has the reputation of being the wildest and coldest locality in England. From Westgate, throughout the walk, the formidable massif of Cross Fell is in view, towering above the small mining community of Wearhead and effectively sealing off the valley.

Westgate, in post war years one of the busiest stations along the branch, possessed ramps which facilitated the tipping of horse and locomotive drawn loads into railway wagons. It also had a platform on the down side and passing loop.

In 1913 the Swinhope Limestone Co. started quarrying half a mile south of the station and built an aerial flight to link the workings to the station yard. The quarry closed many years ago and the aerial flight was demolished about 1950.

The valley, fairly wide at Westgate, soon closes in and cuttings become more frequent.

At Daddry Shield, some distance east of St. John's Chapel there used to be a siding on the south side of the line. The Weardale Lead Co. laid it for some of their nearby, newly found lead seams circa 1918.

St. John's Chapel Station, with its single platform and passing loop was never a thing of beauty; but the village it served was, and still is, very pretty.

The village of St. John's Chapel took its name from the chapel founded there before 1465. It was replaced by the present church with Sir Walter Calverley Blackett footing the bill.

Annually, on the last Friday in May, the Weardale Association for the Prosecution of Felons meets at the village pub, the Kings Arms, to talk and have a meal together. This gathering stems from the beginning of the 19th century when local farmers got together to prosecute any person guilty of a great string of offences from murders, through robbery, burglary, horse, sheep and cattle stealing to burning houses, stealing poultry, robbing or laying waste gardens and serving alcoholic drink on the Sabbath or any other criminal act. Women were eligible for membership of the Association from its inception, circa 1820, when membership was 10/-. The Association recalls the days before there was a rural police force when maintenance of law and order among the lead miners was the responsibility of parish constables.

At one time the Weardale Iron Co. had no less than eight ironstone mines in the area surrounding St. John's Chapel. The first,

Rowantree, was opened in 1863 and others followed until between 1872 and 1876 the mines had reached their peak of production with a combined annual output of 50,000 tons being reached. Thereafter, the industry declined and by 1887 almost all the mines had closed. All this was before the coming of the Wearhead extension.

The mines were situated high on the southern slope of the valley above the hamlet of Ireshopeburn and all were given Weardale names like Foul Wood, Level Gate, Groove Head and Carrick's Level.

Many valuable spars have been mined in this area and at the turn of the century, following the discovery that the hitherto waste fluorspar from the lead mines was valuable as a steel flux and in glass making, there was hope of a revival. Although this has not happened the quest for fluorspar continues on a small scale.

For the last mile the track climbs steadily, eventually steepening to 1 in 78, then 1 in 68, beyond which Wearhead station and sidings come into view.

Sadly the once proud signal cabin, the neat brick engine shed, the turntable and the single platform terminus with its release loop to enable the passenger engine to run round its train have lost their charm. Today the station premises and yard have become the home of a local haulage contractor.

Wearhead station may have lost its bloom but the surrounding heather clad slopes remain as richly picturesque as ever.

It can be cold up there at the back of Cross Fell and is certainly a lonesome place; but to the lover of wild and lonely places where sweeping fells caress the sky, it exhudes an aura of breathtaking beauty.

This short walk has progressed, step by interesting step, into the wild west. It is fitting, therefore, that it should end in real western fashion. At Ireshopeburn what used to be the village school has been converted into 'The Rancho Del Rio', a superbly run saloon famous for its country and western evenings. The fare is finger licking good, the square dancing - toe tapping fine and it all adds up to an interesting and unusual climax to a grand little walk.

29. THE WEATHERHILL AND ROOKHOPE RAILWAY

Length   :   5 miles
Opened :   1846
Closed   :   1923
O/S   :   Sheet 87 - Scale 1:50,000

> *Then in at Rookhope Head they came,*
> *They ran the forest but a miles;*
> *They gathered together in four hours*
> *Six hundred sheep within awhile.*

The verse is taken from the famous Rookhope Ryde, a twenty four verse ballad about the border raid from Thirlwall in Northumberland and Williehaver in Cumberland. The attack was carried out whilst the Weardale men were with Bowes in Barnard Castle in 1569 during the Rising of the North.

Oh! yes. Life used to be tough at Rookhope. In its time it has seen a lot of hard work, bad conditions and poor wages. At one point in its history, because thereabouts were to be found the richest lead yields in Weardale, Rookhope became a lead mining centre.

Rookhope had a smelting mill with a chimney two miles long. It was a surface tunnel cut into the moor with inspection manholes set along it to enable the chimney sweep to do his job properly. His was an important job for the chimney sweepings were of lead and silver. Without that long chimney a fortune could have gone up in smoke.

Lead mining in Weardale ceased at the turn of the century.

The Weardale Iron Co., which was formed in 1846, depended upon Weardale for much of its iron ore, and all its limestone. It approached the Stanhope and Derwent Railway (S. & D.R.) for a line to be built across the moors from Parkhead to connect the mines at Rookhope, Boltshope and Stanhope. The request was refused so the Weardale Iron Co. built its own railways to reach the ore deposits. These were wayleave lines so little is known of their construction. The first part of this system became known as the Weatherhill and Rookhope Railway.

Rookhope lies snugly in the bottom of a valley and it is there that the walk begins. Opposite the village pub, near a public toilet, a path leads northwards to Hilton Row. This unadopted right of way passes some garages, one of which is unbelievably held together with string. Beyond these garages and past some derelict cars the path bifurcates. The way is left and on, through a gate then along a track to the bottom

The ruins of Bolts Law Engine House above Rookhope on the privately owned line from Weatherhill. It may surprise readers to know that this was the highest point ever reached by standard gauge track in Britain (c.1679ft.)

of the railway incline.

At its foot the incline has a gradient of 1 in 6, easing to 1 in 12 at its top. The incline is 2,000 yards long and leads to Redgate Head cutting. Bolts Law engine works and winding house are in the cutting and are well worth inspecting. Built of stone at the top of the incline, the engine works had gantries outside to guide the ropes from the winding drums housed outside. The engine itself was of about 50 H.P. and similar to those fitted to the early steam vessels of that period. The chimney of the boiler house, next door to the engine house, was tall and square and could be seen for miles around. An engine shed large enough to house two tank locomotives for use between Bolts Law and Parkhead was attached to the eastern end of the winding house. A row of houses, standing a little apart, provided accommodation for the people employed there.

From the engine shed the views are superb; and close to the south side of it there is a spring of really clear water, just the job when the incline is climbed on a hot day. Still in the cutting, but a little north of

Looking into Weardale on a winter's afternoon.
The embankment in the centre is the level section
between the bottom of Weatherhill incline and
the top of Crawley incline.

the ruins and on the west side, there is a rock with the face of a man carved on it; but the artist is not known.

For a little while the track, now well and truly in open moorland, continues to northwards before curving to the east along a contour around Stanhope Common. Just before the curve begins a wayside sheepfold is passed on the right and half way around the curve a footpath shoots off to Ramshaw. Between the sheepfold and the footpath the highest point of the line is passed at Hopehead. It is 1,679 feet above sea level and thus has the dinstinction of having been the highest standard gauge railway line ever constructed in mainland Britain. When the line was constructed the mines it served belonged to the Baring family who owned other mines in Rosedale, North Yorkshire. So, in, an odd sort of way, this line is related to the Rosedale line described in chapter two.

As the track takes an easterly course several small feeders of Stanhope Burn can be seen to the south and soon the Burn itself can be seen far below.

One of several Stockton and Darlington Railway stone marker posts still to be found on Weatherhill incline

Although the line was closed in 1923 the tracks remained in situ until 1943. During the years between, a small battery powered car ran up and down it in the shooting season carrying tweedy types to the shooting.

The line, now partly grassed over, continues eastwards along the base of Horseshoe Hill. The walking is easy but the shallow cuttings tend to be waterlogged, even in summer. If speed is of the essence the best thing to do is walk along the tops of the cuttings. But if there is time enough to spare, a close inspection of these long, narrow ponds could be very rewarding. This is especially so in springtime when they are wick with frog spawn, tadpoles and frogs. In fact this stretch of track has become a regular frog colony.

Stanhope Common, a good grouse moor, also harbours a rich variety of other moorland birds. Peewits gather there in large numbers, soaring and wheeling, skylarks abound, filling the air with sweet harmony and frequently the liquid fluting of the curlew directs the eyes towards this lovely bird, which is so much a part of the moorland scene.

117

Bolts Law Engine House almost lost in the snow

Gradually, as it skirts Horseshoe Hill, the track turns from east to south east offering views of Stanhope Burn and Stewart Shield Meadows Farm which is one of the prettiest views thereabouts.

Soon the rough road leading downhill to Stewart Shield Meadow Farm is crossed and the top of a wireless mast comes into view to northwards.

A mile and a half past this mast the Stanhope road is crossed. The bridge has been demolished but the climb down to the road and, once across it, the climb up the other side is easy and trouble free.

Soon the track meets the former Stanhope and Tyne Railway (later to become the S. & D.R.) at its Parkhead depot and becomes as one with it until, about a mile to the south, Weatherhill engine shed is reached. This is the end of the line for this walk; but for the thirsty there is an extension. The road which parallels the line as Weatherhill engine shed is approached, the same one the demolished bridge once crossed, leads downhill to Stanhope, passing Crawley Side en route. There is a pub at Crawley Side but make sure your timing is right because, unlike the walk, it has no extension. Pity, really; but that's life.

30. THE WASKERLEY WAY

Length : 13 miles
Opened : 15th May, 1834
Closed : Weatherhill and Crawley Inclines - 20th April 1951
The rest of the line - 1st May 1969
O/S : Sheets 87 & 88 - Scale 1:50,000

> *I felt its journey, I watched in imagination*
> *Its brown smoke spun with sunshine wandering free*
> Edmund Blunden

The railway promoters were attracted to Weardale by its mineral wealth and the Stanhope and Tyne Railway, floated in 1832, led the way. This notorious line was built to carry limestone from Stanhope and coal from Medomsley. Robert Stephenson was its consultant engineer and its motive power was mixed, 14½ miles being by stationary engines, 14½ by horses and ¾ mile by gravity. The Waskerley Way covers the western and most exciting part of the S. & T. which started at the Crawley Side limestone quarries on the 800 foot contour above Stanhope and ended at the mouth of the Tyne at South Shields.

The rugged geographical features posed tremendous construction difficulties which were exacerbated by lack of precedent for in 1831-2, at the time of the line's conception, railways were still very much in their infancy. It is amazing that, with all the problems of using horses, standing engines and gradients that were so steep that at first they prevented the use of locomotives, the line was ever built. Not until after 1845 were locomotives used; and then on short sections only.

The S. & T. built the whole of the line on land leased from the Dean and Chapter of Durham at rents which, in places, were so exorbitant they eventually led to the railway company's bankruptcy in 1840.

The western terminus of the S. & T. was at the foot of Crawley incline, which, midway down split into two spurs, one to Ashes Quarry and one to Crawley Side lime kilns. The S. & T. projected the route down the Crawley incline to enable lime from Crawley Side kilns, which they owned to be carried to the many depots they had at strategic points all the way to South Shields. All traffic leaving or entering Crawley Side had to be rope hauled up and down the incline by the Crawley standing engine which was sited at the top of it. Some 943 yards long, the incline had gradients as steep as 1 in 8.

119

Waskerley was an isolated railway village on the high moors above Consett. Some buildings remain and people are still here. This view shows one of the houses in its bleak setting

The Crawley standing engine is close to the B6278, which climbs steeply out of Stanhope and makes a good start for the walk.

For one mile and 128 yards the way is up the Weatherhill incline to its engine house. It has gradients as steep as 1 in 12 and, when operative, was worked on the 3 rail principle with a passing loop. Wagons were raised or lowered in sets of 4 or 6. But before this could be effected the ropes of the Crawley standing engine had to be exchanged for the much longer rope of the Weatherhill standing engine, which is now in the National Railway Museum at York.

Once over the summit at Weatherhill the line turned sharply to provide for several long sidings, beyond which the single track wended its way across bleak moorland plateau, at 1,400 feet, on nearly level ground for ¾ mile followed by a similar distance downhill at 1 in 80 to the Parkhead wheelhouse. The whole of this section was originally worked by horses.

For a further mile eastwards from the Parkhead wheelhouse to the Meeting Slacks wheelhouse a main and tail endless rope system was used on the downhill gradient which, for the most part was 1 in 80.

The fossil tree at Stanhope Churchyard

In 1847 a lengthy deviation was provided at a slightly lower elevation and to the south of the original line which completely by-passed the Parkhead wheelhouse. From then on locomotives worked all the way from the Weatherhill engine house to the Meeting Slacks engine house.

When walking this section, an eye must be kept on the B6278, very close on the left. Where it begins to move away, leave the track and join it because ahead a quarry straddles the line. When the quarry closes the walk will be brought through it. Meanwhile use the road to pass the quarry and then cut back over a stretch of moor, rejoin the line north of it, and continue along it. After some very pleasant walking the car park of Meeting Slacks is reached.

From Meeting Slacks the rope was attached for a further 1 mile 453 yards descent to Waskerley on grades from 1 in 47 to 1 in 35.

Waskerley sited on the short level stretch at the foot of the Meeting Slacks incline, assumed real importance after 1845 when the Weardale extension came up from the south.

The long downhill walk to Waskerley through a moorland where physical features are few is absolutely delightful.

121

*Built by the man who built the first Tay Bridge, Thomas Bouch,
and still standing nearly 130 years later. Hownes Gill viaduct
near Consett is 150ft. high and contains
more than 2½ million bricks*

North east from Waskerley the line continued downhill to Nanny
Mayor's self acting incline which was almost two thirds of a mile long
with gradients of between 1 in 10 and 1 in 13. It was capable of dealing
with eight wagons each way.

Mrs. Mayor kept a lineside alehouse.

From the foot of the incline to 3½ miles distant Hownes Gill, the
next obstacle, the grades were gentle and horse drawn 'dandy' carts
were used along it.

Because of the parlous state of the S. & T. finances the company
was not able to build a viaduct across the preciptious, dry gorge at
Hownes Gill. Instead they made do with a cliff cradle arrangement in
which wagons were lowered one at a time for some 147 yards on a
gradient of 1 in 2½. At the bottom turntables enabled the wagons to
be pushed off the cradle for a few yards to be repositioned in the
opposite ascending cradle to be hauled up a gradient of 1 in 3, then
shunted off to await the assembly of the other trucks in the train. This
was by far the biggest bottleneck along the line.

Later a system using funicular railways on each side hauled three trucks at a time, but it was little better than the original system. It was not until 1858 that the bottleneck was cleared by the third owners of the line who did so by building the 150 feet high Hownes Gill viaduct.

The walk down Nanny Mayor's incline, which closed on 4th July 1859, is breezy, easy and gives fine views with Consett ahead on the horizon. But for purists it is a corner cutter, not the Waskerley Way proper. This continues from Waskerley in an easterly direction before swinging south to Burn Hill Junction, where the track going north to Whitehall is taken. The short cut down Nanny Mayor's incline rejoins the Westerley Way just short of where a bridge crosses the track near Whitehall picnic area.

Waskerley is the linchpin of the walk and deserves more than a passing mention. Around this increasingly important station a railway township was created. Rows of back-to-back stone and slate cottages were built, together with a chapel, shops, a club and a school but no pub. So it was that in this isolated moorland township several hundred people lived, worked and played in the boom years of the second half of the last century.

For many railwaymen Waskerley was an arduous but necessary step on the promotion ladder: arduous because living conditions were spartan, the weather usually foul and the surroundings bleak: necessary because these adverse conditions were deemed to develop what good qualities a person had; and to separate the sheep from the goats. Indeed, working on the highest passenger line in England, despite its many drawbacks, frequently bred people of sterling character.

Today this once proud little township is no more. The chapel remains but the shops, the club, the school and most of the cottages have gone. Where once men swore, women gossiped and children laughed and cried today only ghosts remain; ghosts and driving rain and swirling snow and memories.

Leaving Waskerley eastwards along the Waskerley Way the site of Burn Hill Junction is soon reached. Once a station stood there and a depot for military stores; and the now disused line going south from it; straight ahead to Darlington via Crook, was built in 1845. The Waskerley Way, however, is north along this line, through deep cuttings and high embankments, past the Whitehall picnic area and the site of Rowley Station, now rebuilt at Beamish Museum, to join the Lanchester Valley walk east of Hownes Gill viaduct and the

Hownes Gill Viaduct from the north

heavily wooden gorge it spans.

The difficult terrain between Burn Hill Junction and Whitehall picnic area illustrates the problems involved in by-passing Nanny Mayor's incline. That all this was accomplished with picks, shovels and high hopes beggars the imagination.

Where the Lanchester Valley walk cuts across the eastern end of the Waskerley Way, turn left along it to the A692, Castleside to Consett Road and you will have completed a most extraordinary, stimulating and interest filled walk. It's a smasher.

31. THE BRANDON-BISHOP AUCKLAND LINE

Length : 9½ miles
Opened : 1857
Closed : 20th June, 1966
O/S : Sheets 92, 93, 88 - Scale 1:50,000

> *Bobby Shafto's gone to sea,*
> *Silver buckles on his knee.*
> *He'll come back and marry me,*
> *Bonnie Bobby Shafto.*
> *Folk Song*

When George Hudson, the railway King, conceived the idea of building a line from Durham through Brandon and Willington to Bishop Auckland, the main purpose of which was to carry coal and coke, he little thought that his empire would collapse before the line was begun. But it happened.

In the immediate post war years few people would have given much credence to the idea of this line being converted into a pleasant walkway. But it happened. In 1976 the walk, which starts at Broompark picnic area, was opened to the public.

Broompark picnic area is to be found a good half mile west of Neville's Cross as the crow flies but rather more than a mile by winding roads.

From Broompark, which is also the starting point for the Deerness Valley Walk and the Lanchester Valley Walk, the track descends to cross the River Deerness on a footbridge where once the line made the crossing on the now demolished wooden Relly Mill viaduct.

It continues in a south westerly direction, passing through a public open space at Brandon, where reclaimed pit heaps and modern houses hide the track. Brandon was made famous by Robert Grice who wrote *The Bonnie Pit Laddie,* one of the finest novels ever written about a Durham coalfield.

Two miles on, at Sawmills Lane, the track follows the path of the Roman road from Willington to Chester-le-Street and soon the site of Brancepeth Station is reached.

Brancepeth Station was built to serve the attractive estate village of Brancepeth which, in turn, was built to improve the approach to Brancepeth Castle. This mediaeval pile was bought in 1796 by a Sunderland banker and much of it was rebuilt in Norman style by his

125

son. It stands today a magnificent sham.

On the south and west sides of the castle the ground falls steeply into sylvan Stockley Gill. In 1635 timber from the wooded banks of Stockley Beck was used in the building of the navy's first three decker ship, *Sovereign of the Seas*. About 1,400 trees were sent to Woolwich for the ship. Following the Rising of the North in 1569 when Charles Neville, sixth Earl of Westmorland, and Thomas Percy, 7th Earl of Northumberland, made their last attempt to rescue Mary, Queen of Scots from her Tutbury Castle prison, the Brancepeth estate was forfeit to the Crown. However, before the date of the timber sale, Brancepeth had been sold by Charles I to London merchants to clear his debts.

Not long after passing Stockley Gill the view widens and the flattish plain across which the Wear meanders on its northerly journey to the sea, can be determined. To the pedantic this plain is still Weardale but, in fact, Weardale was left behind at Bishop Auckland.

There, west of Trudhoe and neatly set among parkland trees, is Whitworth Hall where Bobby Shafto lived. The Shafto family came to County Durham from Bavington in Northumberland by way of Newcastle, where they became prosperous merchants. In 1648 Mark Shafto, recorder of Newcastle, bought Whitworth Hall and his eldest son, Robert, succeeded him there. In 1661, Robert married Catherine, co-heiress of Sir Thomas Widderington, Speaker of the House of Commons between 1656 and 1658 and Chief Baron of the Exchequer. The name of Robert was common to the eldest son of the house and for four generations they represented in Parliament either the city or the county of Durham. The song *Bobby Shafto* was used as an election ditty; but to which of the bonnie Bobby's does it refer? Ah! That is the question: and the answer is that no one knows.

Away to the south-east the tower of Kirk Merrington church can be seen. Built on a 600 foot high ridge, the church is so prominent a landmark that when the Ordnance Survey people first mapped County Durham in 1856 they used it as a triangulation point.

At Willington the track becomes urban for half a mile or so before emerging once more into a pastoral landscape near Sunny Brow.

Willington used to be the headquarters of Messrs. Straker and Love who leased colleries in the area. They also developed a process which converted poor coal into good quality coke and in so doing made their fortunes.

A footbridge is missing at Rough Lea so a slight detour is needed.

Once there were six brickworks in the four miles long stretch of flat land downstream from Hunwick where an abundance of shale and clay was available for brick and drainage pipe making. Now only one remains. It is at Hunwick and specialises in making fire bricks. The sides of a path from Hunwick to the Wear are retained by rejected pipes. This makes a change from ubiquitous earth; but not for the better.

Silt from the Wear on the northern outskirts of Bishop Auckland has formed a flat, fertile plane in the middle of which sits appropriately named Flatts Farm. The track laces the eastern boundary of the farm aiming for Bishop Auckland which can now be seen ahead, with the Bishop's Palace on the left. The Wear is crossed using Newton Cap viaduct, beyond which the town is reached by bearing right and climbing the hill.

Deerness Valley Walk near Ushaw Moor

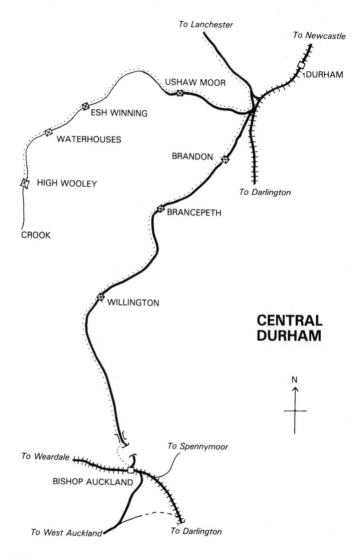

To Lanchester

To Newcastle

DURHAM

USHAW MOOR

ESH WINNING

WATERHOUSES

BRANDON

HIGH WOOLEY

To Darlington

BRANCEPETH

CROOK

WILLINGTON

CENTRAL DURHAM

N

To Spennymoor

To Weardale

BISHOP AUCKLAND

To West Auckland

To Darlington

32. THE DEERNESS VALLEY LINE

Length : 9 miles
Opened : 1858
Closed : 1951
O/S : Sheet 88 - Scale 1:50,000

> *And poets, wits and journalists pronounce*
> *The nineteenth century in prose and rhyme*
> *The most unhappy period of time.*
> *John Davidson*

From Broompark picnic area, created on a former coal stock yard, the walk follows the course of the River Deerness upstream, crossing it five times before climbing steeply up the valley side and over the watershed towards Crook and the Wear valley. Nine miles long, it was opened to the public in 1975 but the two miles ending at Peases West, above Crook, are temporarily out of bounds because of open cast coal mining. Restoration work, however, is in hand and before long it will be possible to complete the walk across a brand new rural landscape. This facelift should enhance the area tremendously.

The Deerness Valley line was built to carry coal from Waterhouse colliery out of the valley. Short branch lines were extended from it to the Brancepeth, Ushaw Moor, Stanley, Hedleyhope and Cornsay collieries, increasing its importance until it became one of the Durham coalfield's main arteries. At the end of a very busy life the line died, aged 93 years, which speaks well of the virtues of hard work.

To Ushaw Moor, almost two miles west of the start of the walk, the views from the track across the river are of a land much of which has been opencasted for coal. It is an area which was for so long almost completely given over to the extraction of 'black gold' that you have to refer to place names to realise that before the River Deerness began to run black other industries thrived there. Two farms, Bleach Green and Sheetburn Mill are reminders of their involvement in processing cloth before the mining was begun.

Once both road and river at Ushaw Moor were spanned by a wooden trestle bridge but this was demolished in the 1960's. Conifers growing on the hillsides thereabouts were planted in 1970 directly into colliery shale and they seem to be thriving.

There is a picnic area on the site of Ushaw Moor Colliery. The pit head gear is still there and pumps below ground are kept working to protect the coastal pits from flooding.

Slightly to the west of the picnic area the track passes under a large bridge carrying a minor road. This bridge was built to carry the main road, B6302 to Flass Hall when it was the valley's main settlement and the road ended there. Nowadays the B6302 continues along the north bank of the river to the head of the valley. The minor road the bridge now carries climbs northwards up the valley side to pass Ushaw College Farm, a Roman Catholic Seminary, which is well sited on a ridge.

Since 1808 more than 2,000 priests have been trained at Ushaw College, many of whom have risen to eminence in the Church. The roll call of famous old students along with some cardinals and archbishops, includes a good many exalted laymen including Francis Barraud the artist who created the famous *His Master's Voice* gramophone trademark.

The college is a self contained community. Its masons cut the stone for a recent college wing from the college quarry. Its carpenters produced its furniture, its painters are responsible for its decoration and food for the students and staff is supplied by its farms. Until the River Deerness came to be blackened with the effects of coal mining water from it was raised hydraulically by the river's own power to fill the college swimming pool. All clever stuff, but the college's chief glory is its ornate and beautifully coloured Victorian chapel.

For more than a mile upstream of Flass Hall the southern bank of the river is pleasantly wooded with a blend of evergreens and deciduous trees. This is a much more aesthetic arrangement than planting purely pine plantations.

The planting of pine plantations for pit props began on the valley sides as long ago as the 1850's; and, really, serried ranks of ubiquitous conifers do little to enhance an area. In these enlightened days as much attention should be paid to the effects of afforestation on the ecology as on the balance sheet; and, thankfully, there are signs that, at last, this is happening.

How evocative of mining is the name Esh Winning! 'Esh' means new and 'winning' means successful shaft or face. This village was once a very important mining village and is well worth a visit if you have timed the walk right, because it contains a cafe, shops and - guess what! - a pub. Many of the villagers have been rehoused and now live in an attractive wooded, hillside estate.

Waterhouses was a colliery village before nearby Esh Winning was thought of. But those days are history now and today the village looks about as dead as its pit. Gone are the colliery, the slagheaps, the terraces and, one suspects most of the miners who worked there.

Less than a mile further up the valley from Waterhouses, at Hamilton Row, the track crosses the river for the last time and climbs through a pleasantly wooded countryside up the steep Stanley incline. When the line was working, a standing engine at the top of the hill hauled trucks up and gravity took them down.

Because of opencast mining ahead, the walk must terminate, temporarily, at remote High Wooley from where there is a minor road going south west to Tow Law. Take it for a mile to join the B6299 where turn left for a quarter of a mile before turning right along the B6298 to one mile distant Crook.

Unlike the Waskerley Way which is used frequently by visitors to the Durham Dales this walk is designed primarily for use by the locals. But don't let that put you off. It is a pleasant and informative walk and people interested in the history of coal mining in particular will be impressed.

33. THE LANCHESTER VALLEY LINE

Length   :   12 miles
Opened :   1st September, 1862
Closed   :   20th June, 1966
O/S   :   Sheet 88 - Scale 1:50,000

> *In the middle of countries far from hill and sea*
> *Are the little places one passes in trains.*
> *Aldous Huxley*

Once again Broompark picnic area is the starting point, only this time the track follows a north easterly direction, cheek by jowl with the main east coast line. This closeness is short lived for within a quarter of a mile the main line curves to the east and Durham City station, and the track swings westwards into the valley of the River Browney. For the most part the track keeps to the south of the Browney although on four occasions the river is crossed.

The line was first built as a single to carry iron ore to Consett but later it was doubled to Lanchester to cater for coal traffic from Langley Park.

As the track curves into the valley and runs close to the river two farms, Quarry House Farm on the far side and Paxter Wood Farm on the near side come into view. Both have semi-circular gingang buildings, inside which, horses once powered machinery pounding an endless circular treadmill.

After a mile or so, on the far side of the river are the remains of an ancient farm, Beau Repaire, where monks used to spend their holidays. Conveniently a bridge spans the river at that point and a footpath leads from the track to it. At present an archaeological dig is being carried out there but once it is complete Beau Repaire will be open to the public.

The countryside thereabouts is agricultural. Cereals are grown on the fertile valley bottom whilst on the steeper slopes sheep and cattle graze. One of the surprising things about this walk is that the valley of the Browney looks much better from the track than it does from the A691 to the north, which does not do it justice. The valley is a coy one, reluctant to release its charms except to those who are prepared to explore it and seek them out.

Upstream of Beau Repaire river and track go their separate ways, one ploughing a straight furrow, the other following a winding course, to meet a good mile further upstream near Witton Gilbert station which once served Langley Park.

Of all the villages on all the walks in this book only Langley Park can claim immortality on the silver screen unless the film fades. For it is often used by film makers to portray pit village life.

A popular game in Durham's mining areas was handball and Langley Park has a purpose built handball wall.

It also has a track side car park.

Between Langley Park and Malton the river and the route of the old railway are never far apart, and at Malton, close to where the track bridges the Browney riverside land has been acquired for use as a picnic area.

The Lord giveth and the Lord taketh away pronounces the Book of Common Prayer. So do the Germans. Their engineers built a benzene works at Malton and German bombers destroyed it in the Second World War.

Malton colliery has also gone but the Germans disclaim responsibility.

Lanchester lies a mile to the north west of Malton. It is named after the Roman fort of Longovicium which is sited on a hill half a mile to the south west. The fort, which encloses six acres and accomodated about a thousand men was built in AD 122 to guard part of Dere Street, the Roman road between York and Hadrian's Wall. It was kept in good repair until the 18th century when the stone was plundered to construct other buildings and little remains.

Lanchester's outstanding building is its Norman built church, All Saints. Roman pillars support the north-aisle arcade and a five foot high Roman altar stand in the south porch.

Opposite the church prosperous looking stone houses edge the wide green of this straggling village.

About all that remains of the railway station is the station master's house now the home of a full time warden.

The building of the Lanchester Valley line caused few engineering difficulties except at one place a mile and a half north west of Lanchester where the line had to cross from one side of Knitsleyburn valley to the other on its climb to Consett. A trestle viaduct, sometimes called Hurbuck after a nearby hamlet of that name and sometimes referred to as Knitsley after the burn it crossed, was built there. Constructed mainly of wood and with thirty six spans of twenty feet each, the structure was seventy feet above the valley floor at its highest, had sharp turns at each end and was extremely fragile looking. By 1915 the structure was in need of major repairs. However the N.E.R. decided, instead, that an embankment would replace it and, at the same time the curve at its south end would be improved at an estimated cost of £16,000. Work was begun that year but because of the war it was not until 1919 that the long embankment was formed. The viaduct was not demolished. It was simply buried by the embankment, the job being completed during 1920.

The walk leaves the track just before the embankment for a prettier route close to the stream, which it follows for about a mile and a half to the second road where walkers turn right along it, over the river, to rejoin the track after a third of a mile.

The former route of the railway east of Hurbuck embankment to Knitsley station, almost two miles away, has been destroyed by opencast mining. Knitsley station, seen over to the left as you walk along the road, away from the burn, is easily recognised despite some vandalism and it is there that the track is rejoined.

A mile west of Knitsley station a link is made with the Waskerley Way to the east of Hownes Gill viaduct and after a further half mile the A692 is reached. This leads directly into Consett.

When the Consett ironworks site becomes countryside again an extension of the Derwent Valley walk will meet the Lanchester Valley walk. So three walks will meet close to Hownes Gill viaducts, there to be served by a new car park. Such interesting developments can do nothing but good.

Lanchester Station

34. THE DERWENT VALLEY LINE

Length : 10½ miles
Opened : For goods traffic - June 1867
         For passenger traffic - December 1867
Closed : For goods traffic - 1962
         For passenger traffic - 2nd November 1953
O/S : Sheet 88 - Scale 1:50,000

Wor Nanny an' me myed up wor minds te gan an' catch the train,
Te gan te the toon to buy some claes for wor little Billy an' Jane,
But when we got te Rowlan's Gill, the morning train was gyen,
An thor wasn't another one gan' that way till seventeen minutes te one.
Wor Nanny's a mazer
Famous Tyneside patter song

What a difference 150 years make! Early in the 19th century the Derwent Valley was a back water. What few travellers ventured up it did so along an abandoned wagonway, which had been built circa 1735 to carry coal from the Pontop Pike area to Derwenthaugh Staiths. The coal wagons were drawn by horses along the wooden rails resting on wooden sleepers and it was by using these sleepers that the itinerants progressed through the mud.

How different it is today! Now the walk along the disused Derwent Valley line is an imaginative blend of natural beauty and historical associations. There are many access points throughout its length and picnic areas have been provided at Rowlands Gill, Ebchester and Shotley Bridge.

The Derwent Valley walk follows part of the old North Eastern Railway which, following a stormy beginning, ran from Newcastle to Consett. The birth pangs were caused by a rival company, the London and North Western, anxious to break the N.E.R. monopoly in the area. The L.N.W. plan was to build the line up the Derwent Valley and continue it past Consett to connect with their own lines to Liverpool. But the proposal was thwarted by an Act of Parliament in 1862 that allowed the N.E.R. to build the line and retain its monopoly.

The walk begins in an industrial setting on the site of Swalwell station and soon passes the site of Axwell Park colliery where, on 6th April 1900, an unusual event took place. A supper was served underground in the gaily decorated Five Quarter seam. The object of the supper was to raise funds for repairs to Whicklam church and it was a well attended occasion.

Axwell Park colliery was the first English one in which three-phase electric current was successfully used to wind coal up a vertical shaft.

Axwell Hall, which looks down on the valley through works chimneys was once the seat of a branch of that powerful north country family, the Claverings, who were colliery owners. Today it is used as a community home for boys.

Few railway walks can have as off-putting a start as this one has: for the first two miles or so there is little to please the eye and much to offend it. Nevertheless it is well worth plodding on because eventually there are signs of improvement.

The improvement begins where the track crosses a lane, Chockburn Ionnen, which for hundreds of years was part of the main drove road from Scotland to Durham. The lane is hazardous but a short detour left along it, then to the right, leads to Old Hollinside, a 13th century fortified house. Legend has it that the Hall was once inhabited by a family of giants who terrorised the neighbourhood. Legend also has it that one of the giants had an underground passage from the house to the Derwent in which he stored his treasure, the value of which increases with the years.

Fact has it that the brews are potent in these parts.

Lockhaugh viaduct, known as the nine arch bridge, carries the track from the east to the west bank of the Derwent. The structure is 500 feet long and built mainly of sandstone with bricks built into the arches. When, in 1907 it was decided to 'doubletrack' the line from Swalwell to Rowlands Gill so fine a job was made of widening the viaduct that, like Ernie Wise's 'wig' it is difficult to see the join.

Soon after Lockhaugh viaduct has been crossed a tall monument comes into view on the left, towering above the trees surrounding the ruins of Gibside Hall, which was built in 1620. The column stands 140 feet high and has a 12 feet tall figure, British Liberty, on top. It was so placed to ornament the grounds surrounding Gibside Hall, grounds landscaped by George Bowes in the 18th century. Work on the monument bagan in 1750 and finished in 1757. For years it was said that the figure held a pot of gold in her hand, there for the taking by anyone who climbed the column. In fact the cup is made of copper and being held upside down, cannot hold anything.

Gibside Chapel has been restored by the National Trust and is open to the public.

By the time Rowlands Gill is reached the scenery has improved to such an extent that all memories of the first two dull miles of the walk have been buried beneath views as pretty as the name Rowlands Gill suggests. When the railway was built there was no Rowlands Gill. It developed later as a commuter suburb. On hot, summer days its children's playground, camping and caravan facilities are usually crowded with pleasure seekers.

The track is lost close to the Lilley brickworks on the northern approaches to Rowlands Gill and picked up again at the viaduct a little further on, the link being a pleasant and easy to follow right of way.

Just before the viaduct is reached the route passes close to the scene of a sensational murder. On 1st November 1855, Dr. Stirling, a young, respected and much liked G.P. was beaten up and then shot. His body was thrown into a nearby plantation. His murderer was never brought to justice. It is said that for many years after the incident the part of the plantation in which his body was found was haunted.

The views from the viaduct, both up and down stream are good.

Soon after crossing the viaduct, on the right close to some farm buildings, is ruinous Friarside Chapel, said to have been founded by a hermit called John, circa 1150. At the dissolution of the monasteries in 1539 this tiny chapel shared the same fate as the great abbeys. Today, battered and with no John, it is still shrouded in mystery, still has its ghosts. These phantoms could have had their genesis in whispered tales told to scare off the curious by the illicit whisky distillers who used to operate along the river bank hereabouts. My bet is that poor Dr. Stirling was done in by moonshiners. Li'l Abner country in staid County Durham! Whatever next! A murdered station master and a ghost train? Forward!

A mile beyond Friarside Chapel a short detour to the left leads over the Derwent to Lintzford where there is an interesting old mill. Built in 1645, it has had a chequered life, first as a corn mill, then a paper mill and, since 1922, an ink works. Lintzford House and the river bridge, both 18th century and built of local stone, are lovely.

Once the river is re-crossed, instead of returning to the track the same way, take the path to the right which will bring you to Lintz Green station, scene of more macabre goings on.

On Saturday, 7th October, 1911, three miners alighted at Lintz Green station from the passenger train from Newcastle at about 10.45 p.m. George Wilson, the station master, saw the train away and was walking to his house when he was shot from an ambush. The three miners, on hearing the shot, ran back and found Mr. Wilson dying in his daughter's arms. The police were called, arrived quickly and searched the area but no one was found. It is thought that robbery was the motive; but no one was ever charged with the crime.

A few years ago a lady who was living in the station house claimed that on wild, stormy nights she would hear the sound of a train passing through the station.

To westwards of Lintz Green station stand two closely positioned viaducts: the first and much smaller one straddles Forgoes Burn and the other, Hamsterley, crosses Pontburn. Hamsterley viaduct is the largest on the old Consett line. It is built of off-white bricks which were made in the Lilley brickworks at Rowlands Gill. Both these viaducts afford fine, birds-eye views of tree tops in the valley far below.

Having crossed Hamsterley viaduct a short detour along the road down to Pontburn is rewarding for on the right, just before the burn is reached, is one of two lodges to the Hamsterley estate, seat of field marshal, the Viscount Gort V.C. who commanded the B.E.F. in France in the early days of the Second World War. He was the grandson of Robert Smith Surtees, the sporting novelist who became internationally famous as the creator of Jorrocks.

In 1909, at a spot roughly midway between the two viaducts and Ebchester, Westwood Station was built. It was the last station to be built on the line and because the buildings were of wood, not stone, once they became too dilapidated to repair the station was closed. This happened in 1942 and Westwood became the first station on the line to suffer this fate.

No sooner has the track straightened after curving to southwards than a lane crosses it leading to ancient Ebchester less than a quarter of a mile away on the right. One of Agricola's forts, Vindomora, lies close to the village which apparently, is unusual because the later Saxons were very superstitious and unusually built some distance away from Roman ruins.

Part of the Norman church of St. Ebba is built of stone taken from Vindomora. The bells of the church strike the quarter hours and on special occasions ring out hymn tunes to summon people to worship.

There is a trackside picnic area at Ebchester and the surroundings are quiet and pleasant.

Shotley Bridge is famed for the German sword makers who came from Solingen and settled there in 1690. They were the country's first steelmakers.

There was a spa at Shotley Bridge with healing waters long before the railway arrived but it never attained the popularity of Buxton or Bath.

Nowadays many hole in the heart operations are performed at Shotley Bridge hospital.

Reporting on the opening of the line in 1867, the Newcastle Daily Journal said 'the scenery opened out by this branch is of a very beautiful description and in the summer will no doubt be much frequented by tourists'. The real beauty then, as now, was trees. They are perhaps more beautiful now than they were when the first train passed by over a century ago; and that can't be bad, can it?

Hamsterley Viaduct

IV Northumberland

Northumberland, the most northerly of English counties is part of the ancient kingdom of Northumbria and is as old as its hills. The Cheviot's were high land before the Ice Age, when the coal measures were still forest; and some of Northumberland's valleys are pre Ice Age.

During the Ice Age glaciers scoured round the Cheviot granite which, together with the North Pennine masses, acted as a barrier to their free flow. Ice deposits left by the glaciers varied from gravel in the north to boulder clay in the south west. The glaciers also helped to mark out the future river courses.

The lie of the land has dictated that the rivers of Northumberland flow from west to east. They are fast flowing and carry mostly different volumes of water between summer and winter, as can be seen by the generous arches of their bridges. Game fish, trout and salmon, abound in them but they are far too fast flowing to harbour coarse fish like perch, pike and roach. The murky waters of the Tyne at Newcastle give little indication of the real Northumberland. The sparkling waters of the North and South Tyne are much more in keeping with the spacious green rural vales through which they flow before, a few miles west of Newcastle, they become heavily polluted. The rivers of Northumberland, the sparkling Rede, the twisting, trout filled Coquet, the Till, which turns northwards by Chillingham, long famed for its wild cattle, the Aln and the Tweed, beloved of salmon fishers, are, with others, an important part of the lure of that lovely county.

The Cheviots, that long range of moorland heights and lonely glens, which straddles the county's western margin and through which the English-Scottish border runs, is a land of spacious solitudes. Although lacking in rugged grandeur the bare, brown heights nevertheless hold great attraction for those who seek lonely places. These desolate haunts of the sheep and the curlew are devoid of either shelter or habitation. For in this inhospitable environment even the shepherd's cottages are tucked away in deep, winding valleys.

In pre-Roman days the first settlers made a precarious livelihood along the foothills of the Cheviots where they lived in circular huts and scooped-out enclosures.

When the Romans, under Agricola, pushed north they built a network of roads which greatly eased communication problems and from which they could patrol the area and suppress any disaffection.

Saxon freebooters, plundering Danes and the all conquering Normans all left evidence of their presence.

Throughout most of the 13th century the kings of England and Scotland were fully occupied dealing with rebellious barons. Then, when Alexander III of Scotland died and Edward I decided to meddle in the Scottish succession, it marked the outset of 50 years of Border warfare with the systematic despoiling of monasteries, castles, churches and farms.

Centuries of Border strife followed, as grim, old castles, pele towers and scarred masonry testify. Today more than 300 fortified sites, in all shapes and sizes, have been recorded in Northumberland.

Even more enduring than its characteristic ruins, Northumberland's ballads tell of its turbulent growth.

In the Middle Ages few of the feudal barons of Northumberland had home-farms where they could utilise labour so, unlike those in other parts of the country, they drew rents from their tenants in grain and money instead of unpaid work.

The church land owners, on the other hand, required 2 or 3 days field service every week and also hired workers by the season or the day whenever it suited them.

From as far back as the 7th century cattle and sheep rearing have been a very important facet of Northumberland's economy. The leather and the wool they provided were vital to English trade; and by the end of the 13th century Newcastle-upon-Tyne had become the leading English exporters of hides.

Many drove roads score the county from north to south, worn by countless Scottish drovers bringing home-bred cattle to the great markets of Newcastle-on-Tyne, the Midlands and London.

Border Leicesters and black-faced sheep are to be found on the higher Cheviot 'heafs' whilst black cattle, Red Devons and Lyloes, graze the upland pastures. Fresians, Charollais cross-breds, known locally as 'charlies', and occasional herds of Jerseys are confined to the lower pastures.

There is no great horse or pony tradition in Northumberland.

The natural building material is stone: hedges are rare. The most famous monument in Northumberland is a wall. Hadrian built it.

Mining and quarrying have affected Northumberland hardly at all and where this occurred restoration work is in progress. Colliery waste is being grassed over or used for road metal.

The tracks of disused railway are being lifted.

Today modern Northumberland, while preserving its ancient heritage, is catering for a new and altogether friendlier invader - the tourist. It has a lot to offer him, or her, like mountains and moors and sparkling streams, rough pastures and water meadows, woodlands and sand beaches. Oh yes! the natives are friendly and the beer is good.

35. THE WYLAM AND WALBOTTLE WAGGONWAYS

Length : 6¾ miles
Opened : Circa 1748 - Wylam Waggonway
Closed : 11th March, 1968 - Scotswood, Newburn and Wylam
Line
O/S : Sheet 88 - Scale 1:50,000

And hurrah for our fellows, who in their need
Could fashion a thing like him...
With a heart of fire, and a soul of steel
And a Samson in every limb.
Alexander Anderson.

Circa 1748 the Wylam Waggonway was built to transport coal from Wylam to the Keels at Lemington because at Wylam the river was too shallow to accommodate the keels.

By 1780 another waggonway, the Walbottle, was operational. It was part of a system of waggonways owned by the Duke of Northumberland to carry coal from his Walbottle pits to the coal staithes on the Tyne at Lemington. This branch incorporated part of the Callerton system which had been built before 1767, leading from Holywell colliery some 3½ miles north of Lemington. Coal was carried along these waggonways in high sided wagons drawn by horses or rope hauled along an inclined plane. At Lemington keelmen were employed to tranship the coal to sea going vessels downstream from Newcastle bridge.

By the beginning of the 19th century an extensive system of horse-drawn or rope hauled waggonways had developed on the north bank of the Tyne. However they were not able to meet the increasing demands for the cheap transportation of coal in bulk and this led to the rapid development of locomotive engineering in the north east of England.

In 1876 the Scotswood, Newburn and Wylam railway line was built on the site of the wagonway between Scotswood and Wylam. It provided an alternative route along the north bank of the Tyne to the earlier built route from Newcastle to Carlisle which, on leaving Newcastle, crossed the Tyne at Scotswood and crossed to the north bank at West Wylam junction. The S.N. and W. was taken over by the North Eastern in 1883 having been worked by that Company from the outset.

The bridge which carried the north bank line over the Tyne at Wylam. It is the oldest of its kind in Britain and was the model for Sydney Harbour Bridge, amongst others

A number 605 bus from Marlborough Crescent serves Wylam and there is a car park behind Stephenson Terrace on the north side of Wylam bridge. This bridge provides an interesting start to the walk as it was the model on which Sydney Harbour bridge was based.

George Stephenson's father was a fireman at Wylam colliery and George himself was born at High Street House, less than half a mile east of Wylam, on the 9th June, 1781, and spent the first eight years of his life there. The building is still there today and is looked after by the National Trust.

On 9th June, 1881, to celebrate the 100th anniversary of Stephenson's birth, a procession of locomotives was held between Newcastle and Wylam, passing his birthplace.

For a period, in 1966-67 the Newcastle and Carlisle route between Scotswood and Wylam junction was closed and during that time all traffic used the north bank line and passed Stephenson's birthplace.

A commemorative bronze tablet was unveiled at High Street House on 8th June, 1929, by the Lord Mayor of Newcastle. It had been erected by the Institute of Mechanical Engineers of which George

Stephenson was first President and by the North East Coast Institute of Engineers and Shipbuilders.

The first two miles of the route and High Street House are in Northumberland. The rest of the walk, because of boundary changes, is in Tyne and Wear. The going is good and the outlook very pleasant and rural. From Blaney Row the way is first along the north side of the road through the Tyne Riverside Country Park, then across the road and along a footpath on the south side of the old waggonway to Water Row, past the 'Boathouse' and the site of Water Row Pit to Newburn Bridge, the halfway point.

From Newburn Bridge a route continues eastwards to Scotswood but becomes increasingly industrialised. But this is abandoned for the rural waggonway northwards to 3½ miles distant Black Callerton. The way is left across the level crossing and right along Station Road to High Street, then along Church Bank to the church where Stephenson was twice married.

The path is now west along Church Bank to the war memorial, then up a flight of steps along Hareside Path and Berkley Terrace to rejoin the route of the old wagonway through Walbottle Dene. In crossing the dene the route drops to the site of New Winning and then climbs up the other side, keeping to the right of the stream. Once a small waterfall is passed the way is right along a narrow footpath, past the site of Duke Pit, to rejoin the wagonway across a grassed area.

The route continues west, then north along Grove Road, past the line of Hadrian's Wall, across the B6528 and along a footpath on the west side of the Engine Inn, keeping to the line of the Walbottle Moors wagonway to the A69(T) road.

The A69(T) is a very busy road so it is better not to cross it. Instead, go westwards for about 300 yards and use the underpass which will bring you to Dewley Road. Walk eastwards along it for some 300 yards to Cut End and you are back on course. Cut End is named after a cutting made for the wagonway.

Once over the signposted stile at Cut End the wagonway and the footpath following it bifurcate, the north western branch passing the Dewley Pit area, where Stephenson lived in the 1790's, and continuing northwards to Greenwich Moor while the north eastern branch goes to the Black Callerton and Holywell Main areas. One of the pits in the Black Callerton area was Dolly Pit where Stephenson worked as a brakeman.

This latter route crosses Walbottle Moor, an area of open heath,

145

before turning north eastwards to rejoin the wagonway to the next field boundary. The way is now along an embankment until both footpath and wagonway split again. One branch leads north, the other to the east; and the choice of routes is yours.

This half of the walk, northwards from Newburn, is all decision making, isn't it? Don't let this put you off for the section is brimming with interest.

The northern branch continues in that direction along a slight embankment parallel to the field boundary, then across a second field to the B6342, east of Lough House. The path continues on the far side of the road, past Broomhall Farm, to the Black Callerton road along a well defined embankment.

The eastern branch goes along an embankment on steeper gradient, diagonally across the field to the field boundary, where the footpath turns left, away from the wagonway, to a kissing gate leading to the Stamfordham road. The path continues on the line of the wagonway for 150 yards along the road to the right, where it crosses a stile and goes along an embankment. Now the path follows the original route of the wagonway diagonally across the next few fields but, apart from some spoil heaps, little of the wagonway can be seen because of ploughing.

The path joins a minor road going northwards to Black Callerton.

The northern ends of the three branches previously mentioned are all linked by a minor road from Callerton Lane Ends to Black Callerton: so, if you are seeking a little variety, why not go up one and return down another? The third can be tackled at some future date.

These wagonways, while having a great historical interest are for the most part, still rural and fun to explore.

36. THE ALSTON-HALTWHISTLE LINE

Length : 13 miles
Opened : 17th November, 1852
Closed : 3rd May, 1976
O/S : Sheet 86 - Scale 1:50,000

> *We kissed at the barrier; and passing through*
> *She left me, and the moment by moment got*
> *Smaller and smaller, until to my view*
> *She was but a spot.*
> *Thomas Hardy*

Had the charming lady in the poem departed from Alston on or after the 19th October 1870, she would have had a very enjoyable ride for the 13 miles long journey northwards to Haltwhistle is delightful. Had her departure point been Haltwhistle on the 19th July 1851, she could have been on the first passenger train to use this branch line. For on that date the 4½ miles from Haltwhistle to Shafthill were open for passenger traffic. On the 5th January 1852, the eight and a half miles from Lambley to Alston were opened for goods traffic but not until the Lambley viaduct was completed could the entire branch be opened. Authority was given for the line to be extended from Alston, over the watershed, to Nenthead but this section was abandoned. In 1870 another unsuccessful bid was made for a line from Alston to Stanhope, but the watershed was never crossed.

Following a general rule that railways stick to the lowest route, the Alston to Haltwhistle line keeps close to the beautiful South Tyne, which it crosses to enter Haltwhistle station. It is a charming route along a sweetly rural vale, not unlike Upper Teesdale, where lush green banks are perfumed by wild flowers, trees arch delightfully over rushing, brown waters and wild birds congregate in profusion.

Soon after crossing Knarburn, half a mile N.W. of Slaggyford, the disused line and the course of the Roman road, the Maiden Way, linking Kirkby Thorne in Cumbria with Carvoran fort near Hadrian's Wall, keep each other company.

Another companion, the A689, is a martyr to snow: the weatherman only has to mention the word and the road is blocked with deep drifts. For this reason despite the heavy losses the branch line was making in the days before Mr. Beeching did a hatchet job on unprofitable lines in 1963, the Alston branch was kept open because there were no alternative methods of transport in the area in severe winter weather.

147

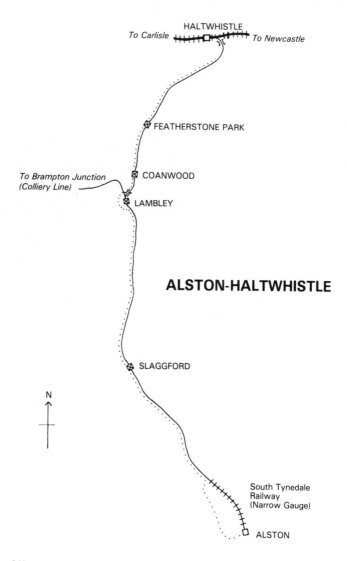

To Carlisle — HALTWHISTLE — To Newcastle

FEATHERSTONE PARK

To Brampton Junction
(Colliery Line)

COANWOOD

LAMBLEY

ALSTON-HALTWHISTLE

SLAGGFORD

N

South Tynedale
Railway
(Narrow Gauge)

ALSTON

*When the Alston branch closed the station was taken over by a
Preservation Society who have laid a narrow gauge track
which currently extends about 1½ miles to the north*

For several years under various Ministers of Transport, the branch line was subsidised and in 1973 a decision was made to close it once the road had been improved. The closure date was set for 1975 then postponed; but the reprieve was short lived and now the steam engines and the diesel multiple units that replaced them have become part of the history of a line that is no more.

It was the lead mining around Alston that first attracted the railway pioneers of the 1840's and caused the line to be built.

In 1911 the journey from Alston to Haltwhistle took 35 minutes. In 1971, sixty years later, the journey took 34 minutes. That's progress for you!

Right up to its closure the Alston line was regarded as the last genuine branch line to remain in full time operation through the rural part of the north east. But towards the end its running and maintenance costs became so high that one railway official said it would be cheaper to carry each of the line's regular passengers by chauffeur driven Bentley! Little wonder it closed.

37. THE BELLINGHAM-RICCARTON JUNCTION LINE

Length : 25 miles
Opened : 1st July, 1862
Closed : 15th October, 1956
O/S : Sheets 79 & 80 - Scale 1:50,000

> *Past cotton grass and moorland boulder*
> *Shovelling white steam over her shoulder*
> *Snorting noisily as she passes*
> *Silent miles of wind bent grasses.*
> W.H.Auden

This grand walk begins very pleasantly in Bellingham and ends at a lonely outpost in the Cheviot hills some five miles inside Scotland. It follows the route of the Border Counties Railway, which was built when railway building was in its prime, linking Hexham with the Hawick-Carlisle line on a bleak, windswept hillside eight miles north of Newcastleton.

Bellingham, pronounced Bellinjam, is a large, agreeable place in an elysian setting below some of the most barren of the Northumberland moors. It was the ancient capital of the North Tyne and has lived through troubled times. The roof of its 12th century parish church, St. Cuthbert's, was built of stone as a guard against the firebrands of Border reivers, the marauding bands of cattle thieves who raided along the English-Scottish Border in the 16th century.

The North Tyne flows broadly past Bellingham and the disused railway line keeps close to its northern bank all the way to Kielder Water. From the outset the countryside is enticing and the walking good because much of the old track is overgrown with grass. At this stage of the walk there is nothing to suggest the barren landscape ahead. The North Tyne, youthful still, glides gently across deep, brown dubs and spills over shallows, its stone bed clear and clean. The tree lined banks enhance the surrounding well-husbanded farms. The North Tyne, when the warming sun shines, is, on the suface at any rate, all harmony and contentment.

Interest in developing a railway link along the North Tyne valley from Hexham began in 1845 but it was not until 29th November 1853, that the Border Counties Railway's prospectus was placed before Parliament. The idea was for a single track line to be built from the Border Counties Junction near Hexham, to Bellingham Burn, near Plashettes, where coal was being worked from stream sections and shallow pits. The line, 26¾ miles long and having ten intermediate stations, was to be an outlet for coal from Plashettes and iron stone from the Bellingham area. The necessary Act of Parliament was granted in 1854, the line was built during 1855 and opened in 1856.

It had always been the intention of the Border Counties Railway to make a junction with the planned North British Railway line from Hawick to Carlisle so, in 1856 the B.C.R. submitted plans to Parliament for its *'Teviotdale'* section from Belling Burn to be extended to join the N.B.R. near Belser Mill bridge.

At the same time the Carlisle Liddesdale and Hawick Railway made counter proposals for a branch from Riccarton to Belling Burn, the temporary B.C.R. terminus near Plashettes.

The very day the North British's Border Union Railway between Hawick and Carlisle was opened the Border Counties Railway ran its first service to Riccarton Junction.

It had been hoped that the B.C.R. would provide competition for the main line from Newcastle to Edinburgh; but this was not to be. The steeply graded route precluded fast running, making it an unattractive route for Anglo-Scottish passengers.

The Plashettes' coal now being transported to the Tweed Valley woollen mills was also a disappointment because it proved to be an unsuitable steam coal and had to be marketed for domestic use only.

However the picture had a bright side. An unexpected, alternative source of income was found, moving livestock to and from Newcastle mart.

Beyond Falstone the Border Forest Park increasingly impinges on the track bringing a claustrophobic sameness to the scene. Established in 1955, it is the largest of Britain's planted forests and is formed by six principal forests of which Kielder is one. This huge forest park has brought life and prosperity to an area that was dying of poverty. But with it has come a dreary sameness of surroundings and a lack of variety and interest in the serried rows of conifers, mainly Sitka spruce.

Beyond Kielder Water some six miles of track lie at the bottom of Kielder reservoir, three quarters the area of Windermere and one of the largest artificial lakes in Europe. Therefore it is advisable to have a means of transport available at this point to transport you to Kielder village, where the track can be rejoined.

Before continuing from Kielder towards the Scottish border a short

The fine castellated viaduct at Kielder is one of the few bridges to be scheduled as an ancient monument

walk back along the reservoir is most rewarding. For there, on the edge of the village, is to be found the magnificent masonry Kielder viaduct which because of its seven skew arches and unusual decorative work was preserved in 1969 by the Northumberland and Newcastle Society and is now maintained by the Northumbrian Water Authority. The road it was built to span is now drowned and the lower level of the viaduct's piers has been encased in concrete and partly submerged but most of this fine structure can still be seen. Although the line it carried was single track the viaduct is broad enough to have carried double track with ease. It really is a spanker.

Kielder station, renamed Kielder Forest Station in 1948, used to have a special 'tree siding' to handle saplings brought from Aviemore.

Shortly after leaving Kielder Forest Station the track breaks free from the regimented avenues of spruce and crosses a flatland of coarse wind-bent grasses and stunted trees. At times the conifers encroach but the line avoids them, skirting them for a while before making a bee line for Deadwater station, on the Scottish border.

Peel Fell, the most westerly spur of the Cheviots, lies to the north of Deadwater. At its foot the North Tyne bubbles out of the ground to begin life as a sluggish stream, a dead water, hence the border station's name.

Walking in coniferous plantations is not everybody's cup of tea but for the first half mile or so of the line's journey into Scotland that is the way of it - unless the road along the valley bottom is taken as far as the edge of the forest, where the track can be rejoined close to where a self-conscious bridge crosses it half way up the valley side.

From now on the way is airy, climbing along a bare hillside with good views, across the narrow valley to southwards, of Foulmire Heights. Steadily the track climbs the valley side then slices through a deep cutting close to its brow and crosses the Bonchester Bridge-Canonbie road at Saughtree. The four arched viaduct has been demolished but crossing the road presents no problems and within a quarter of a mile Saughtree station, with its protective walls of fir trees is reached.

Saughtree station was probably the most isolated railway halt in Britain. Towards the end only one train in each direction stopped there on three days a week!

Next stop Riccarton Junction; and for most of the way the track climbs steadily up the side of Upper Liddesdale, giving fine views of the Larriston Hills on the far side. En route, several gates bar the way, each with its distinctive method of opening. The gradient eventually levels out near the summit and the track goes through a curving cutting in which huge colonies of tadpoles, in season, live in muddy pools.

Once through the cutting all is changed. The embankment immediately ahead soars above a steep and narrow gorge on the sides of which thousands of young spruce grow. On all the surrounding steep sided heights more young firs grow. Today these once bare grassy slopes look like stubble covered chins. Not all that many years hence a thick beard of ubiquitous, evergreen softwood will completely envelope them.

A bare line cuts through the little firs along the steep slope over to our left. It marks the route of the Hawick-Carlisle line some three miles short of Whitrope Summit, the highest point on the line between Carlisle and Edinburgh Waverley. Clearly Riccarton Junction is close. Two more twists in the line and there in the middle distance, is all that remains of that remarkable out-post in the hills.

Before the North British Railway Company built a station in the wilderness, two miles from the nearest road, and named it Riccarton Junction there was nothing but bleak moorland.

Like Topsy, Riccarton simply grew and grew. It began as an exchange platform where passengers travelling along the Border Counties Railway could connect with main line trains. Then a six engine shed and a carriage depot were built. Initially six cottages were built to house the railway staff but as the years progressed and permanent way and operating personnel were based at 'the junction' more cottages had to be built to house the growing population. At its peak Riccarton Junction had a population of about 100 dwelling in some thirty-three houses.

All Riccarton's eggs were in one basket. Its sole purpose was to look after the trains crossing the bleak Borderland hills. It was completely cut off from the outside world and relied entirely on the railway for its livelihood. The community pub was a building on the platform, which later became a well-stocked grocery store. A post office was established in a corner of the waiting room and, later, a telephone kiosk was provided on the platform.

The station master was also the Provost, postmaster, head warden, fire master and hall keeper.

There was a primary school with two teachers and the school hall was also the venue for the community's occasional dances and special functions. At first church services were held in the engine shed and later were held in the station waiting room.

Whenever anyone was ill an engine was despatched to Newcastleton, to fetch a doctor who would travel to his patient on the footplate; and since Riccarton had no burial facilities corpses had to be taken by rail to Newcastleton cemetery for burial.

In the station's early days a huge aspidestra dominated the refreshment room where tea and hot scones were served in a truly domestic atmosphere. Towards the end fewer than half a dozen people per week availed themselves of this splendid service.

Now little remains of that once proud community. Most of the houses have gone, the innermost third of the bay has been filled with rubble and nature is surely reclaiming the ground the railway took away from her all those years ago.

Once whistles of steam engines on the Waverley line could be heard twenty minutes before they reached 'the junction'. Now the only whistles are from blasting winter winds.

Today the only humans living in that lonely place, with its ghosts and its memories, are a few forestry commission workers.

The last railway man left years ago.

Some people may prefer to treat the section from **Bellington** to Deadwater as a complete walk. The distance, 20 miles less the six underwater miles in the middle, makes a respectable 14 miles of pleasurable walking.

From Deadwater to Riccarton Junction the distance is five miles but, since steps have to be retraced to the Bonchester Bridge-Canonbie road at Saughtree the distance is boosted to eight enjoyable miles, making this section a respectable walk.

The whole walk is interesting and full of variety. It simply screams to be tackled. So go on - treat yourself - have a go. You won't regret it.

A smaller remnant of forgotten railways is this baggage weighing machine on the platforms at Riccarton Junction. This remote and fascinating place has suffered badly from official vandalism and little remains to be seen

APPENDIX

A detailed examination of wildlife on a section of Hudson Way Educational Nature Reserve: Market Weighton-Spring Wells

This reserve, approximately 2.1km long, is a fine example of one good use to which a disused railway track can be put. Managed by the staff and pupils of Market Weighton Secondary School on behalf of the Yorkshire Naturalists Trust and in co-operation with the Technical Services Department of Humberside County Council it is at once a traditional 'nature walk' and a nature study centre.

The reserve is open to anyone but serious study groups and school parties should inform the Head Teacher of Market Weighton Secondary School of their proposed visits; and everyone must obey the rules. There are only two and they are loaded with common sense:-

(1) Please observe the country code
(2) Remember, 'take nothing but photographs: leave nothing but footprints'.

For the benefit of school parties fifteen marker posts divide the track into 100m lengths and information sheets and questionnaires are available for each one. The one from the start to the first marker post, for example, encourages pupils to investigate the plant colonisation of the cinders on the northside of the trackway, and to look for horse tails, descendants of the giant species which grew in swamps millions of years ago and became coal. The question 'what kind of trees can be seen here?' is asked and the answer, 'ash' is given.

The reserve is rich in flora and fauna, with a variety of trees, shrubs and bushes providing good cover for the wide variety of ground plants growing there. Over thirty species of birds may be seen in the reserve at any one time, depending on the season.

The species and flora lists given below have been prepared by the masters and pupils of Market Weighton Secondary School and serve to show how lush with natural things this disused line is. They also show how, with a little mutual co-operation, a forward looking school and an enlightened County Council are germinating in the minds of children a greater awareness of their surroundings and their under-standing and, hopefully, subsequent love of our declining wild life.

The Hudson Way educational nature reserve is a triumph, well worth repeating throughout the land, for its benefits both to mankind and to its flora and fauna are bouldless; and it all began with a disused track.

Birds

Barn Owl	S	Blackbird	A	Black Headed Gull	W
Blue Tit	A	Brambling	W	Chiffchaff	S
Coal Tit	A	Collared Dove	A	Common Gull	W
Crow	A	Cuckoo	S	Dunnock	A
Fieldfare	W	Goldfinch	A	Great Tit	A
Green Finch	S	Green Woodpecker	S	House Martin	S
House Sparrow	A	Heron	W	Jackdaw	A
Kestrel	A	Lapwing	W	Linnet	A
Long Tailed Tit	A	Magpie	A	Mallard	W
Mistle Thrush	A	Moorhen	A	Pheasant	A
Redwing	W	Robin	A	Rook	A
Short Eared Owl	W	Siskin	W	Skylark	S
Song Thrush	A	Spotted Flycatcher	S	Starling	A
Swallow	S	Swift	S	Teal	W
Tree Sparrow	A	Waxwing	W	Whitethroat	S
Willow Warbler	S	Woodccock	S	Wood Pigeon	A
Wren	A	Yellow Hammer	A	Yellow Wagtail	S

A-All Year   *S-Summer*   *W-Winter*

Flora

Alder: Ash: Bird's-eye Speedwell: Birdsfoot Trefoil: Black Medick: Blackthorn: Bramble: Burnet Saxifrage: Cleavers: Coltsfoot: Common Sorell: Common Vetch: Creeping Buttercup: Creeping Cinquefoil: Creeping Thistle: Crosswort: Cudweed: Daisy: Dandelion: Dog Rose: Elderberry: Fairy Flax: Field Bindweed: Figwort: Fools Watercress: Forget-me-not: Great Willow Herb: Harebell: Hawkweed: Hawthorn: Hedge Wound Wort: Hogweed: Hoptrefoil: Horsetail: Ladies Bedtrain: Mate Fern: Marsh Willow Herb: Meadow Cranesbill: Meadow Pea: Mignonette: Mouse Eared Chickweed: Mouse Eared Hawkbit: Nipple Wort: Ox-eye Daisy: Pineapple Weed: Ragwort: Ribwort Plantain: Rosebay Willow Herb: Salad Burnet: Scabious: Selfheal: Small Toadbox: Stonecrop: Toadflax: Thyme: Wall Speedwell: White Campion: White Clover: Willow: Yarrow.

The Country Code

Guard against all risk of fire
Fasten all gates
Keep dogs under proper control
Keep to the paths across farmland
Avoid damaging fences, hedges and walls
Leave no litter, take it home
Safeguard water supplies
Protect wild-life, plants and trees
Go carefully on country roads
Respect the life of the countryside

The cottage where George Stephenson was born next to the wagonway at Wylan

BIBLIOGRAPHY

Baker S.K.	Rail Atlas of Britain	Oxford Publishing Co.	1977
Duerden Norman	Portrait of the Dales	Robert Hale	1978
Goode C.T.	The Wensleydale Branch	The Oakwood Press	1980
Jones Edgar	The Penguin Guide to the Railways of Britain	Penguin Books	1981
Lidster J.Robin	The Scarborough and Whitby Railway	Hendon Publishing Co	1977
Redman Ronald	Railway Byways in Yorkshire	Dalesman Books	1979
Ridley Nancy	Portrait of Northumberland	Robert Hale	1965
Speakman Colin	A Yorkshire Dales Anthology	Robert Hale	
Warn C.R.	Rural Branches of Northumberland	Frank Graham	1975
White Peter	A Portrait of County Durham	Robert Hale	
Whittle G.	The Railways of Consett and North West Durham	David and Charles	1971
B.R. Regrouping Atlas and Gazetteer		Ian Allan Publication	1972

ACKNOWLEDGEMENTS

Top of the list for my grateful thanks is David Bell who not only took the excellent photographs which grace this book but also shared my adventures along the disused railways and kept me on the right track.

David joins me in thanking the following people for their help and encouragement in the preparation of the book and without whose help it might never have been written. Mr. T.J.Edington, Information Officer, National Railway Museum, York; Mr. R.J.Lundie, Senior Recreational Footpath Officer, Humberside County Council, Technical Services Dept., County Hall, Beverley for the conducted tour of the Hudson Way and other similar projects aimed at popularising disused railways in North Humberside; Mr. J.Moor, T.D.C. Eng., Director of Technical Services and Mr. Ingles, Senior Public Rights of Way Officer, both of Humberside County Council for their enthusiasm: Mr. John Miller, Countryside Commission, Leeds; Mr. Alan Mesham, Footpath Officer, Northallerton for assistance with the North Yorkshire branch lines; Mr. Ryon, Countryside Officer, County Hall, Durham for guidance regarding the County Durham branch lines; Mr. Tony McDonald, National Parks Officer, Hexham for similar help regarding the branch lines in Northumberland.

The verse from the Geordie song *'Wor Nanny's a Mazer'* is quoted with the kind permission of J.A.Windows Ltd., Newcastle.

Information regarding the Educational Nature Reserve on Hudson Way is reproduced by kind permission of Mr. C.Norman, Education Officer, Yorkshire Wild Life Trust.

We should also like to thank Mr. Campbell Richardson co-proprietor, with his lovely wife, of the Grapes Hotel, Newcastleton, Roxboroughshire, Scotland for being so forthcoming with information about Riccarton Junction, his birthplace and where he was raised.

We are also indebted to the helpful staff of the following libraries: Central Library, Newcastle upon Tyne, Darlington Public Library, Crown Street, Darlington, Hull Public Library, Hull Central Library Service, Hull.

Extra special thanks must go to Stephen Barker, Ron Dodsworth and Neville Shaw, good companions all, who have proved that, as on honeymoon, when walking in such good company you can have tremendous fun without bursting into laughter.

My grateful thanks also go to Marjorie Bell, who translated my handwriting into type.

If we have omitted anyone it is unintentional and we apologise.

Printed by Carnmor Print & Design,
95/97, London Road, Preston, Lancashire.